LAST DITCH

&

LAND OF MY FATHERS

BY

DAVID IAN RABEY

with expository essays edited by
Lara Maleen Kipp and Piotr Woycicki

Print ISBN 978-1-0685688-4-8

Published by
Llyfrau Cambria Books, Wales, United Kingdom.
Cambria Books and Cambria Stories are imprints of Cambria Publishing Ltd.
Discover our other books at: www.cambriabooks.co.uk

Anyone wishing to perform either of the plays published in this volume should contact the dramatist at this address: davidianrabey@gmail.com

Dedication

To those who made these happen...

Cover credits:

Lynx hexagram motif designed by Carys Wise.

Last Ditch photos by Hubert Sikorski (featuring: on front cover: above: Roger Owen, Katherine Taylor, Adrianna Wanda Czajczynska, Ella Thomas, Rachel Barwise; clockwise: Katherine Taylor, Iona Greenslade*, Roger Owen, Kuba Pawelczak, Oliver Riordan, Oliver Turner; except * by Shannon Black. On back cover, above: Iona Greenslade).

Land of My Fathers photos by Keith Morris (featuring: on front cover: Oliver Morgan-Thomas and company; Huw Blainey. On back cover: Oliver Morgan-Thomas, Huw Blainey).

On *Last Ditch* and *Land of My Fathers*

David Ian Rabey's plays fairly zip along, dancing between myth and modernity, laced with high ideals, fine poetry and pitch-dark jokes. Watching them on the stage, I was moved, amused, and horrified in equal measure. It is a joy to have them on the page too, our chance to wallow in their conceptual ambition and high-wire wordplay. - **Mike Parker**

These two plays provide a devastating account of what can only be called the contemporary condition. *Last Ditch*, while wholly original, could also be seen as recapturing and reshaping Beckett, connecting existential concerns with a powerful critique of capitalism, war and slavery, all formed into a radically new language of pauses, hesitations and sudden explosions. *Land of My Fathers* is a stunning indictment of war and what war produces and encourages; here the reference points are *Heart of Darkness* and *Apocalypse Now,* the terror is of 'going native', and all this is taken through a further twist in the contexts of Afghanistan and Iraq, but with reflections on Wales and Welshness at its heart. Who, these plays encourage us to ask, is making whom do what? Where might we find hope amid a desperation that we have been trained to accept and turn into the banal? - **David Punter, Professor of Poetry, University of Bristol**

On *Last Ditch*: This beautiful, dark, urgent and driven play explores and pushes the boundaries of both language and stagecraft. It is propelled by the existential imperatives of our times. Its rage against unchallenged authority and uncontested privilege is genuine and necessary, as are, thankfully, its insistence on the primacy and salvation of love and respect. Maybe, it whispers, all is not, yet, lost. That's to be celebrated. - **Niall Griffiths**

I have enjoyed David Ian Rabey's plays very much indeed, over many years, both on the stage and on the page. His writing is uncompromising, robust and poetic with a rhythm all its own. His characters can be brutal and dangerous or courageous and moving. His awareness of many different traditions informs the theatre he creates; always political, argumentative, engaged, sometimes violent and startling. I was privileged to see the first production of *Last Ditch* and found the mysterious music of the writing arresting and enthralling, an imaginative tour de force that addresses our own dangerous times and all the times to come. - **Patricia Duncker**

Rabey's theatre is not a stage but a space, bare and uncompromised. He peoples it with figures 'on edge', in what feels like a dystopian future but very soon becomes visible as our Now, exposed. His own native heath is itself on an edge, where the Black Country overlooks westward an ambivalent borderland where ancient British (i.e. Welsh) placenames lie unsleeping: Wenlock, fair monastery; Kinver, hound hill...

In *Land of My Fathers*, such more mainstream names are parodied and mocked by characters Welsh themselves; and for a finale the soul-arousing anthem of the title surges forward on full throat as though to canonise a hideous onstage act of psycho-political violence. And there's a deeper irony in play in this piece: where British 'civilian' asymmetricals, blooded as Welsh squaddies in West Belfast, are now corporate agents visiting their own oppressive history on the new 'Welsh' of Iraq and Afghanistan.

When, in an early sequence in *Last Ditch (Anghrefn yng Nghymru)* we hear the same impotent line surfacing spontaneously from character to character, the only words they can say, we feel we're hearing language itself on the edge of extinction. Yet paradoxically both these pieces climax in an apocalyptic celebration - in *Land of My Fathers*, a 'visit' to a subterranean sculpture gallery in progress, confronting us with images of mythic stature, of a primordial atrocity that can only be imagined, but a defiant act of creativity nonetheless; in *Last Ditch*, an anarchic global Rapture, mediated via phantasmal video-imagery and the conjuring voice of a creature half-feline half-man.

For either of these two pieces 'Play' is too comfortable a word. 'Enactment' might come closer. And that, after all, is what the Greek word 'drama' literally says. The author himself has personally hinted that these, for practical reasons, may be the last he writes. I hope not. - **David Rudkin**

On **Land of My Fathers:**

Rabey's subject is masculinity under small restraint […] The potent physical presence of three men is only half of what Rabey as director has made. The foreground screen plays out in front of a large screen. Piotr Woycicki has assembled a rich flow of imagery for his digital scenography […] A giant heart throbs in all its raw anatomical substance. The eye of the lens circles around a Minotaur. […] If *Land of My Fathers* has a line to encapsulate it is: 'if you don't know what you stand for how do you defend it?' *Land of My Fathers* eschews strict naturalism but also avoids a soup of symbolism […] Iestyn, Cai and Owain make their own journey into the twenty-first century hearts of darkness […] Rabey's script demonstrates, the dark hearts are not spatially and geographically limited. They beat, universally, within every human ribcage. - **Adam Somerset, *Theatre in Wales* website, 12/05/2018**

On **Last Ditch (Anhrefn yng Nghymru):**

[Rabey] knows form, structure but also knows that theatre is elementally one thing. It is human energy unleashed across space. *Last Ditch* plays out as a taut sequence of bouts of movement, sound, gesture […] *Last Ditch* fits into an older tradition of Wales: "A sense of the fantastic", as Simon Harris once wrote, "the development of an avant-garde and anti-naturalistic theatre, as evidenced by such companies as Brith Gof, Moving Being, Volcano and Y Cwmni/Fiction Factory." […] Spectres from theatre's history, Toller and Kaiser, haunt the Castle Theatre. But if an artwork is held in an embrace of its predecessors it is also itself and Rabey has given it a flourish of personal signature […] The energy that propels *Last Ditch* is propelled by its visual élan. It starts with the players themselves. Richard Downing has devised plaster-white faces with jagged cracks. The result is as disquieting as it is distinctive. The third part unveils a change to startle. The curtains have been used throughout for projections. A new character, the Lynx, […] takes the lead. He sets off a sequence of visual bravura. Monumental statues shake themselves into graphic motion. They begin with Owain Glyndŵr in Corwen and include lumpy figures from Italy's fascist era. [Aberystwyth's] Castle Theatre is a few hundred metres from Mario Rutelli's seaward-looking women of stone. They too join the action. […] The theatre that we know of goes back two and a half thousand years and Lurking Truth and its friends are faithful to the art. 'An entity is composed of opposing forces' says a character. Theatre […] is the art of that illustration. - **Adam Somerset, *Theatre in Wales* website, 30/09/2023**

On Rabey's previous published plays, ***The Wye Plays***:

Fierce, muscular texts in the spirit of Artaud and John Clare. - **Iain Sinclair**

A writer who combines a ruthlessly exploring intellect with a superb, at times shocking, dramatic instinct. His characters are as memorable as those in early O'Casey. - **Brendan Kennelly**

On ***Lovefuries***:

**** Stylish and stylistically challenging work … a riveting and explosively physical performance. - **Susan Conley, *The Irish Times***

CONTENTS

Director-Dramatist's Foreword to *Last Ditch* by *David Ian Rabey*

What happens in *Last Ditch*?

An angel of anarchy recruits a gang of broken renegades who aim to counter a slide into cosmic suicide, by triggering the most spectacular series of events in the history of the world, to affect a worldwide cultural and spiritual transformation.

Scene synopsis:

In Part 1 (Nigredo) we encounter:

Tanwen, who attends a peaceful protest with her girlfriend Lowri. They are brutalized by riot police.

Sion, a drug addict, forces money from his friend (or relative?) Catrin, to feed his heroin habit.

Dyfrig, a man who uncharacteristically resolves to speak out his inmost feelings of love for a woman.

Beti, a partially sighted woman who is reduced to becoming a carer for her husband Joe, a war veteran, after he suffers a stroke.

Tanwen is interrogated and tortured by a policeman, Ronan. He taunts her with the news that Lowri has died during her torture and interrogation. Nevertheless, Tanwen refuses (as did Joe) to betray her colleagues.

We see Ronan in contrasting contexts: his first meeting with his partner Aisling, their engagement in light-hearted sexual playfulness. We also see his subsequent subsidence into PTSD and depression, his toxic behaviour towards Aisling, and her ultimatum that he should leave her house.

Joe knowingly elicits and encourages Beti to euthanise him. His death presages the first appearance of Boneblack, who releases and gathers Joe's memories and processes Joe into death; a procedure which Boneblack will subsequently perform, for other characters when they 'break black' from their last moments.

In Part Two (Albedo) we encounter:

A gathering and convocation in a dimension beyond the conventional human perspective. Boneblack is joined by Rubato, Anhrefn, and M, to consider the parlous state of the tenancy of the world by human beings, whom they call 'mayflies' – a term which reflects their innate limitation of perspective ('They live so briefly'), yet also their innate potential to surprise ('They MAY fly'). M is contemptuous of humans and their damage and wants to accelerate their cosmic suicide. Anhrefn, aka 'Annie', thinks that unjust suffering can be resisted, that the 'mayflies' deserve further chances of wider options. Rubato and Boneblack defer.

M intervenes in human affairs by approaching an influential politician, Wearhead, whom he engages in a Faustian pact, which gives Wearhead short-term but extensive worldly power. In exchange, M afflicts Wearhead, and their children, with terminal disease. M also presides over the deaths of Sion (by overdose) and Ronan (by suicide). M observes the traumatized responses of Catrin and Aisling, whom he also infects.

In reaction, Annie determines to make her own intervention in the human realm, defying Boneblack's misgivings.

Aisling encounters Dyfrig in a cancer ward, where Dyfrig awaits the specialist's diagnosis of his wife. They express differing views of the times remaining to them, respectively. Beti encounters Catrin in a care home, where Beti is a patient and Catrin works as a nurse. Beti identifies a futility in their prospects and insists Catrin should help her escape. As Tanwen is released from prison, Annie materializes before her.

In Part Three (Citrinas) we see:

Annie gives Tanwen an overview of events so far, and exhorts her to find a 'Firm', gather a nucleus of suitably desperate followers who also have nothing to lose. Tanwen recruits Beti, Dyfrig, Aisling and Catrin, all united by their experiences (or prospect) of loss. Annie is underwhelmed, but arranges for Rubato to appear and address them all. Rubato brusquely dismisses their traumatized, self-pitying paralysis and preaches a gospel of self-overcoming.

In defiance of Aisling's terminal diagnosis, she and Catrin fall in love, and express their feelings. Annie suggests a means by which Tanwen may be able to draw the tumour out of Aisling, but warns that the process, if not completed, carries the risk that Tanwen may harbour it herself. Dyfrig is outraged by observing this initiative and demands that Tanwen do the same for his wife, but Tanwen is too exhausted. Dyfrig shares with Beti his regret at vengefully telling Tanwen that he wished she was the one who was dying. Aisling discovers she is cured. Beti professes her faith in Tanwen's mysterious intimations, in the time available to them.

In Part Four (Rubedo) we see:

Annie guides Tanwen into a human summoning of The Lynx, 'Guardian doorman at the portal of the possible', to assist them in creating 'The Most Spectacular Event, In The History Of The World'. Though sceptical, Tanwen consents; The Lynx materializes and stirs himself into triggering the simultaneous worldwide animation of statues, who rise up in opposition to various human forms of control and repression. The Firm lead other protesters against reactionary responses of attempted containment by riot police; Beti sacrifices herself, and her fearless death provides a decisive crisis of loyalty for at least one member of the police. Annie exults in the worldwide upsurge of chaos and tells Boneblack that she envies the mayflies in their newly unfettered erotic liberation; she mischievously suggests that this has given her some new ideas.

Tanwen confronts a shattered and deserted Wearhead, intending vengeance. Annie appears to Tanwen a final time and persuades her to leave Wearhead to their former supporters, who now realize that Wearhead is a liability. M attempts a final initiative, which Annie challenges, by exposing and overcoming his fundamental fearfulness. Annie makes a timely intervention, to make a contrary direct appeal to the imaginations of the audience members. M's principal weapon is fear. Annie counters: that humans are intrinsically different, but not therefore essentially separate. It is not that their life has no meaning, but that M is – like some humans – denying the possibility of meaning and the possibility of making it together. Crucially, she disarms him through a startling non-destructive initiative: a demonstration of both active and significant difference, and erotic inclusivity.

Dyfrig proclaims himself ready for death, but Boneblack refers him to the beauties of continued worldly existence. Aisling and Catrin are euphoric and intoxicated with idealistic future possibilities potentially springing from the world's opportunity to "reset"; though Catrin observes that not everyone will be willing to embrace infinite change. Back on the streets, Tanwen interrupts and confronts the remaining representatives of repressive violence, still engaging in unjust brutality, and offers them a choice, which extends beyond obedience to totalitarian and plutocratic power.

Objectives and contexts:

2019-20: I was seizing probably my last opportunity of production facilities and support to write and stage a large-scale epic play, in purposeful defiance of a climate of cultural, theatrical, political, and spiritual contraction.

2023: All of the above, but in a different social context; more urgently, in the wake of ensuing and impending events.

Backstory:

When Lockdown 1 hit in March 2020, I was working on a first production of the play, scheduled to have its first showing as a departmental production (my last, before my retirement from teaching in August 2020) for Aberystwyth University Department of Theatre, Film and Television Studies, and performed in Theatr y Castell. The Arts Centre were selling tickets (most of the four nights were sold out), we were at dress rehearsal. Then COVID lockdown hit. We had to stand it all down…

…and it started coming true. I was shocked to see some of the darker imaginings of *Last Ditch* proving prophetic and happening, in some form: police conduct before and during the Black Lives Matter protests and the Sarah Everard vigil (and since); an unprecedented global event which made conventional daily life grind to a halt, for many (COVID and lockdown); and, in advance of the events in Bristol and elsewhere in Summer 2020, the play imagines a startling form of worldwide 'statue wars' (incorporating significant local details, such as Mario Rutelli's victory statues in Aberystwyth). The play did (and does) not feel any less timely; if anything, more urgent. Hence the drive to perform it, in an even more ambitious, purposeful, spectacular form.

Formal influences and guiding principles:

The drama of:

Howard Barker: particularly, *The Forty* (written 2006, staged by Aberystwyth TFTV & Lurking Truth 2011, 2014): forty precisely distilled elliptical playlets depicting characters at crisis points, the seizing or decay of an impulse.

debbie tucker green: particularly, *ear for eye* (2018), its introduction of a wide range of characters who sometimes deploy similar phrases in different contexts.

Alistair McDowall: particularly *Pomona* (2014, staged by Aberystwyth TFTV 2016), its succinct yet mysterious introductions of various characters (some of which may not be, or do not remain, human), whose surprising points of contact only become apparent later.

David Rudkin: particularly *Merlin Unchained* (written to be staged by Aberystwyth TFTV at Theatr y Castell, 2009), an explosive epic which passes between worlds, which startlingly collide.

The writing in other media of:

Alan Moore: particularly *Jerusalem* (2016), in which beings and ghosts from a conventionally extra-perceptual layer of existence decisively intervene in the flat plane surfaces of human events; and *Promethea* (1999-2005), in which the apparently catastrophic 'end of the world as we know it' offers the opportunity for further positive possibilities.

Grant Morrison: particularly *The Invisibles* (1996-2000), a gnostic narrative development of a boundary-shattering psychoactive 'voodoo doll universe' intended to closely map (and potentially influence) our own; and his reflection on practice, *Supergods* (2012).

Artworks:

Damien Hirst's exhibition, *Treasures from the Wreck of The Unbelievable*, which I witnessed at the 2017 Biennale in Venice, and his other work exhibited at Houghton Hall in 2018. Hirst's comment in the Netflix documentary about the *Treasures* exhibition was also salutary: 'What makes you believe in things is not what's there – it's what's not there'. In Venice, I also encountered the similarly awesome installation, *The Horse Problem* by Claudia Fontes. I pay homage and tribute to these inspirational works – and make more mischievous references to an eclectic range of other statuary – in *Last Ditch*. These are intended in the spirit of respectful and playful citations, as when a jazz musician incorporates into his explorations of one song a reference to another. On this phenomenon, Geoff Dyer observes:

> All art is also criticism. This is most clearly so when a writer or composer quotes or reworks material from another writer or composer. All literature, music and art '*embody an expository reflection on, a value judgment of, the inheritance and context to which they pertain*' [Dyer's italics, quoting Steiner] (Dyer 2012: 186).

Meri Wells's ceramic creature The Lynx (which I own, and which resides in my house): I reimagine this as a gruff, self-dramatizing but benign genie/animal avatar who can hold position at a border and intercede and communicate in ways that human beings can understand.

Development:

I was inspired by the idea of angels. I am not religious in any institutional or literalist form, but that has not prevented other existentialist artists (such as those already acknowledged, but also Gaiman, Kushner, Wenders, Hicks-Jenkins, Brith Gof) entertaining the proposition of observing perspectives and forces, positioned not as saviours but as principles, presenting temporal perspectives beyond those available to humans. As Morrison observes, adding time to the world picture is like adding perspective to a painting (Morrison 2012: 275). 'Faith' in its various forms is a big part of making theatre: the invocation of the mysterious and the unseen, as well as (and by) what is visible and audible. The imagination offers us 'an innate knowledge of other life', which is how Howard Barker defines 'soul' (Barker 2016: 62). I think it is possible to discern benign and malign forces at work within our world, and these go by many names. I am not convinced that materialism can account for all forms (and values) of life, so the other stuff must contain (if not comprise) what we might call 'spiritual'. So: Hark, The Herald Angels Sing: like Scott Walker arranged the strings.

I profoundly distrust sentimentality in art, but I am not opposed to melodrama, in what I regard as the best sense of that term (my own): an artwork which is grounded in the terrain of realism, but which develops its narrative in ways which purposefully and surprisingly challenge the dominant terms of realism and engage the active moral will of the audience.

Every good drama requires a conflict with a negative necrophilous principle, which I identified with the simple letter 'M' (the Cymraeg word 'Manylion' inspired a linguistic *trompe l'oeil*, suggesting a pride of raging power in English/yn Saesneg and translating as 'details' yn Gymraeg – an apt *nom de guerre* for a devilish confidence trickster). This character offers the audience the promise of a silent 'clean and peaceful' post-human world, on the condition of abdication from responsibility and effort, through cosmic suicide. In retrospect, M might be summarized using Morrison's terms: he is 'what happens when you let bad stories eat good ones' and 'turn all your dreams to nightmares' (Morrison 2012: 368).

Alan Garner claims that 'anthropology shows that no human society is known to have existed without a sense of the numinous, in the form of ancestors, spirits, gods' and that 'prayer may be seen as dialogue with the numinous, and we may need to give the numinous form in order to speak to it, whether as a bearded old man, a rock, a pool, a cave, a bone' (Garner 2024: 181). Or, I would add, as characters in a theatre. My late friend Brendan Kennelly defined prayer as 'anger at what is, and longing for what may be': even, or perhaps especially, when it does not, cannot, expect an immediate response. Grant Morrison's concept of the hypersigil –a dynamic feedback loop which aims to create significant change and alter reality in accordance with intent, influencing wider perceptions and behaviours (see Morrison 2012) – might be considered a secular form of this: an extended imaginative project which ideally aims to impact on, and fruitfully disrupt, the conventionally perceived and given rules of existence. It would accord with Garner's insistence that creativity is not a job, but a state of being involving 'service to something beyond the self', and 'in this broad sense, it partakes of the religious' (Garner 2024: 174).

I began with experiments in writing observational scenes of terse extremity, separate but overlapping snapshots of increasing human desperation in conscious experience, as initial intentional ingredients towards a dramatic sigil, which then might be earthed and condensed by a structure. Here I was inspired by Mike Parker's *On The Red Hill* (2019) which constructs a matrix of liberation from elements, seasons, compass points and participant identities. As my mythic (and Jungian) crucible, I chose the four alchemical principles and stages of transformation:

Nigredo: a blackening: a rendering down into decomposing putrefaction, despair as a preliminary to awareness of the shadow.

Albedo: an illuminating whitening: a division into two opposing principles, to be subsequently coagulated.

Citrinas: a fiery kindling of internal (rather than reflected) light.

Rubedo: the integration of opposites, transcendence, individuation, irreversible renewal, reunification.

Charging this structure with my deliberately wildest gnostic imaginings, the rest of the play surged out with astonishing speed and detail, moving from the observational to the visionary, in Garner's terms (*ibid.*: 157).

To stage this 'spiritual-political extravaganza', we would need profoundly suggestive effects, on every level, which could combine to overwhelm all previous sense of possibility. Fortunately…

Enter Craig Shankster, a researching practitioner of acousmatic sound: sound which one hears, and feels, without seeing, or otherwise readily identifying, its cause. Craig would compose and perform, live in the theatre space, a score which would support each performance's mysterious sense of the suggestive but indefinite.

Enter Piotr Woycicki, who had alerted me to the remarkable possibilities of his digital scenographic work, during our previous collaboration on my play *Land of My Fathers* (2018). The wilder the verbal cues which I posited, the more evocative and original the protean shapes Piotr found, to give form to their energies. These extended from the pictorial unfurling of each character's varying emotions, as they died, to the slow-motion bone smash of disfiguring violence, to the adhesive splattering gush of grief at a suicide, to The Lynx's triggering of 'The Most Spectacular Event, In The History Of The World'.

Enter co-director Oliver Turner - and, as performers, his fellow members of the 2022-3 MA in Performance and Scenography cohort (Oliver Riordan, Jade Roberts, Katharine Taylor), joined by some members of the original 2020 team (Rachel Barwise, Connor Elliot, Iona Greenslade, Ella Thomas) departmental graduates (Shannon Black, Laura Bragg, Maddy Cook, Adrianna Wanda Czajczynska, Kuba Pawelczak, Matthew Sole), locally based practitioner Ritz Wright, and original founder members of Lurking Truth since 1986: Roger Owen and Richard Lynch.

Oliver Turner comments on the unusual form of the ensuing dramatic text:

> The first thing you notice when opening a David Ian Rabey script is how beautiful it looks on the page. Words are arranged in a picturesque landscape of double-spaced size-12 Times New Roman font, like a form of computerised pointillism. It's somewhere between Shakespeare and

> abstract, illustrative poetry. You start to read… The second thing you notice is that, to an outside eye, if you use this landscape as an instruction manual for how to deliver the text, it doesn't make any sense… **but it does**. There **is** a rhythm here. Somewhere. Or rather it's rhythmically arhythmical. This bizarre effect means that it's quite difficult to pre-visualise anything as a director. Textual clues do exist, but I soon figured out my preferred strategy was to discover scenes along with the performers in the rehearsal room. Sometimes the rehearsal process can feel like transcription of the dramatist's intention into reality. My experience on this occasion was far more organic and immediate, and therefore more democratic. This may well have been heightened by my position as a fellow cast member. David had set us a riddle without figuring out the solution. It was a collective effort between the two of us, the rest of the creative team and the cast to unscramble it. Along the way, we were going to find as many different ways as possible of delivering 'This is the beginning of the end. / Isn't it?' as we could.

Charmian Savill has observed in conversation how *Last Ditch* presents pantomimic performances in a Beckettian landscape:

> The initial Nigredo/'N' scenes of the play present scenes of characters being knocked down, of renegade souls drying up: depicted in distilled and minimal ways, with deliberate gaps, which the audience member is invited to fill in from their own imaginations. Then the Albedo/'A' scenes show that another spiritual perspective is achievable. The ensuing varying scenes of manifested loss, grief and resistance nevertheless show the characters slowly building up. There's a sense that it is not arbitrary whom Annie appears to: it is earned by Tanwen, in contrast to another hundred people who might not choose to see her, or engage. It is the image and promise of a couple, erotically entwined in a wilderness, which is at the heart of the story, which offers the confidence to explode out of the tyranny of the Now.

'To be truly radical is to make hope possible rather than despair convincing' – Raymond Williams, *Resources of Hope* (1989)

REFERENCES:

Barker, Howard (2016) *Arguments for a Theatre* (fourth edition). London: Oberon.

Dyer, Geoff (2012) *But Beautiful.* Edinburgh: Canongate.

Garner, Alan (2024) *Powsels and Thrums*. London: 4th Estate.

Morrison, Grant (2011, 2012) *Supergods*. London: Vintage.

FURTHER VIEWING:

Telfer, Pete (2024) *Behind The Last Ditch.* Online documentary (42 mins) about the 2023 production. Culture Colony. https://culturecolony.com/en/media/video/behind-last-ditch accessed 21/04/2025.

LAST DITCH
(ANHREFN YN NGHYMRU)

A spiritual-political extravaganza

Last Ditch (Anhrefn yng Nghymru) was first rehearsed at Aberystwyth Theatr y Castell January-March 2020, as a second-year practical production by Aberystwyth University Department of Theatre, Film and Television Studies, with the following company:

Cast:

ANHREFN /'ANNIE'	IONA GREENSLADE
M	AIDAN DAVIES
BONEBLACK / THE LYNX	MATTHEW EVANS
RUBATO / SION / RIOT POLICEMAN	DAVE WILLIAMS
TANWEN	IMOGEN COWGILL
RONAN / CONTRITE RIOT POLICEMAN	AMY JONES
AISLING	ANNA KARCZMARCZYK
DYFRIG	LUKE HALLAM
LOWRI / WEARHEAD	KAROLINA SALASA
CATRIN	RACHEL BARWISE
BETI	ELLA THOMAS
JOE / RIOT POLICEMAN.	MINA VLASTARI
GWENLLIAN	ELINA OTSAMO

Director: DAVID IAN RABEY

Assistant Directors and Understudies: CONNOR ELLIOT and ELINA OTSAMO

Scenographers: KIRSTIE ADDIS, JAKE CHRISTIE, DAISY COATES, ELLAJEN PRICE, JASMIN ROBERTS, CARYS WISE, working with the direction of RICHARD DOWNING and BECKY MITCHELL.

Live Soundscape composed and performed by CRAIG SHANKSTER (silenceinsound.co.uk)

Deputy Stage Manager: HOLLY GIBSON

Vocal Training: LARA MALEEN KIPP

Trailer Filming and editing: GOSIA WENDT

The production was shut down at the stage of first dress rehearsal by the University's COVID lockdown.

Last Ditch (Anhrefn yng Nghymru) was subsequently staged 29-30 March 2023 at Aberystwyth Theatr y Castell, as a co-production by Aberystwyth University Department of Theatre, Film and Television Studies (in celebration of their 50th anniversary) and Lurking Truth / Gwir sy'n Llechu Theatre Company, with this slightly revised text, and the following company:

Cast

ANHREFN/'ANNIE', an Angel of Anarchy IONA GREENSLADE

M, a Fearful Djinn OLIVER RIORDAN

BONEBLACK, a Gatherer of Memories OLIVER TURNER

RUBATO, the Genius of Time / RONAN, a Man who Takes His Work Home / RIOT POLICEMAN

MATTHEW SOLE

SION, a Bedevilled Young Man / CONTRITE RIOT POLICEMAN

KUBA PAWELCZAK

TANWEN, a Woman on a Journey KATHERINE TAYLOR

AISLING, a Grieving Lover ADRIANNA WANDA CZAJCZYNSKA

DYFRIG, a Cautious Man ROGER OWEN

LOWRI, a Seasoned Protester / WEARHEAD, an Opportunist

JADE ROBERTS

CATRIN, a Care Worker — RACHEL BARWISE

BETI, an Undefeated Woman and Wife — ELLA THOMAS

JOE, a War Veteran and Husband / RIOT POLICEMAN — RITZ WRIGHT

GWENLLIAN — SHANNON BLACK

THE LYNX, a Liminal Guardian — RICHARD LYNCH

Co-Directors: DAVID IAN RABEY and OLIVER TURNER

Assistant Directors and Understudies: CONNOR ELLIOT and SHANNON BLACK

Live Soundscape composed and performed by CRAIG SHANKSTER (silenceinsound.co.uk)

Digital Scenography and Animations: PIOTR WOYCICKI

Lighting Design: STEPHEN GRIFFITHS

Deputy Stage Manager: MADDY COOK

Assistant Stage Manager: JONNO CASSELL

Lighting Operator: LAURA BRAGG

Costume, Make-up and Props Design: SHANNON BLACK

Scenographic Guidance: RICHARD DOWNING

Programme and Poster Design: IONA GREENSLADE

'LAST DITCH' Logo Design: CARYS WISE

With thanks for support to: Dr Kim Knowles; Professor Jamie Medhurst; Professor Simon Banham; Becky Mitchell; Chris Stewart.

The action of the play takes place sometime next week: in Cardiff, West Wales, London, worldwide and beyonder.

Names appearing without dialogue indicate an active silence between those characters.

Words in (brackets) are intention only and not to be spoken.

Prologue: THE ARGUMENT inspired by a conversation with Charmian Savill.

PROLOGUE: THE ARGUMENT

'DYFRIG' ACTOR: Each day you're startled slightly:
By some *uncommon* sense:
A dividing combination
Routine is now pretence;

Winds challenge your balance,
Draw you into a silence;
The stars pull you outwards,
Uproot your compliance;
And you're feeling the large,
being trawled by the small
It's a pivot in time
That's a rise AND a fall:

You can't sum it up, and you can't pin it down;
At the back of your mind, on the tip of your
tongue,
There's an underground stream in which
something could drown,
Something pulled out the hooks,
where your certainties hung.

Its extent and its texture
We can't follow through;
We don't yet have the language

With which to pursue;
We don't yet have the knowledge
With which to construe,
But you look into it
And it looks into you.

'ANNIE' ACTOR: It's the leap you've not taken,
It's the thing you've not thought,
It's the instinct dismissed,
It's the feeling you fought,
It's the sensual pleasure,
That you wished you'd been taught:
It's a flickering presence,
That won't stay, or be caught.

'TANWEN' ACTOR: The moon and the sun
The waves and the stars
Are what people observe,
As they trace their own scars;
They're confounded and cured
By the wrench of the light,
That can darken the day,
And can shine in the night.

'LOWRI' ACTOR: It's how light can come crashing
Through the glass that we make,
Bringing depth, doing damage,
To show form, and to break

'CATRIN' ACTOR: Windows, books, statues, paintings
Seek a time to be seen
Are they shallow or solid?
What's the depth in a screen?

'AISLING' ACTOR: They're contained or containing?
Or confusing the two?
Are we shedding our skins?
Can a fiction be true?

'BONEBLACK' ACTOR: There are shapes in the spinfoam
There's a presence in space
And in time, complicating,
enhancing, all trace
Figures fuse, and enfuse,
they confuse subterfuge,
And they slide out the frames
of the ways they've been used.

'M' ACTOR: Like some skeletal driftwood
Turning into a mare,
Like a house with no windows
But with blind eyes that stare,
Going up in a tree,
going under the bed,
Mocking those that are living,
coming back as the dead

'RUBATO/RONAN' ACTOR: Shadows cannot redeem
But we question all truth.
We can't change you, or save you,
But we won't stay aloof.

'M' ACTOR: What is worse, that we watch you?
Or perhaps that we shan't?

'BONEBLACK' ACTOR: What is worse, that we stop you?
Or perhaps that we can't?
That we can't change what happens?
Or that neither will you?

'ANNIE' ACTOR: That what you do is crucial?
That all this might be true?

'BETI' ACTOR: So, then, what do you wish for?
What would you like to see?

'SION' ACTOR: What's your hope? What's your dread?
Some new way to be free?

'JOE' ACTOR: Or perhaps these are tangled,
Interwoven like silk:
Shot through with angles
That won't fit into talk -

'CATRIN', 'AISLING', 'TANWEN', 'BETI', 'DYFRIG', 'SION', 'JOE':

We are here to raise spirits
Draw some patterns in dust;

ALL:

Not resigned, not defenceless,
We respond when we must.

PART I: NIGREDO

Kuba Pawelczak and Matthew Sole as Riot Policemen; Katherine Taylor as Tanwen. Photos by Hubert Sikorski.

N1:

TANWEN: This is the beginning of the end
Isn't it?
Can we do this?

LOWRI: We can't not.

TANWEN: *(love and pride, not resentment)*
You're making me do this.

LOWRI: Not true.

TANWEN: You won't be sorry –

LOWRI: Oh yes. We will.

TANWEN: You know I'm –
(*a profession of love, cut short brusquely)*

LOWRI: Yes. *(Horror seeps into them both.)*

TANWEN: I shall let them down.
I shall let you down.

LOWRI: Not true. Breathe deep.
(Beat)

I won't make the same mistake.
(as on some previous occasion she remembers…)
(wry, jaunty) Keep me alive till morning? *(Kiln-fired:)*
WE: Can be better than this. I can't bear this.
(Intake of breath)
When we dream:
the dream comes, from us.
When the enemy appears in our dream:
the enemy, also comes from us.
But we can step into it. Surprise it. And tear off its mask.
Right now. *(They breathe deep)* Hold on:
NOW

N2:

SION: (*Strung out. Frayed. Twitching. Pacing. Wild-eyed*) I can't bear this.
(*Startled alarm at a sudden numbness:)* I've lost my face. (*Desperate*) I CAN'T BEAR THIS.

DEALER: Not true.
You need to have this. *(offers drug)*

SION *(has no money.)*

DEALER: *(shrugs)* You hold on. *(Leaves.)*

N3:

(AISLING & RONAN pass each other on the street. AISLING turns back.)

AISLING: Hey.

RONAN: Hey.

AISLING: Hey.
You have sad eyes.

RONAN: (*shrugs, laughs*) Hey.
(*They both hold the gaze*)

N4:

(Two people, find a place to sit.)

(Pause.)

DYFRIG: This is the beginning of the end.

Isn't it?

(Breathes deeply)

I won't make the same mistake. *(as on some previous occasion he remembers…)*

You know…?

You KNOW

I'm completely in love with you.

GWENLLIAN: Oh

Don't

We can't

I can't

DYFRIG: We can't not.

(They are still.)

N5:

(Elderly couple, pursuing separate simple activities)

JOE: (*sudden alarming discovery*) I CAN'T
I CAN'T
CAN'T
CAN'T *(He turns off radio, and collapses)*

BETI: *(long-suffering, irritated)* Hold on.
(Now:
registering the unusual seriousness of his situation)
Hold on.

JOE: (*Gasps: then manages the words:)*
This is
The
Beginning
Of
The
End
Isn't it? (*She shakes her head in horror.)*
(JOE looks into her:
with an insistent, remorseless honesty) ISN'T IT?

N6:

(TANWEN & LOWRI face off against Riot Police.)

LOWRI: (*to TANWEN*) Now.

(*LOWRI & TANWEN stand firm.*
RPs do the same. RPs raise truncheons.
LOWRI and TANWEN gasp.
RPs give order; advance; strike.
LOWRI AND TANWEN fall howling.)

TANWEN: You can't just … You can't.

1st RP: Not true. (*Strikes TANWEN*)

LOWRI: We have to do this.

2nd RP: Not true.

LOWRI: You're making us do this.

2nd RP: Not true. (*Strikes LOWRI*)

TANWEN: NO. YOU CAN'T

1st RP: Can't not. (*Points to TANWEN*)
You're making us do this.

(*Looking at TANWEN, he strikes LOWRI again. TANWEN howls.*)

2nd RP: We do what we must do.

(Indicates LOWRI, to TANWEN)

1st RP: Not true. (*Approaches TANWEN, looks at LOWRI: pauses: strikes TANWEN)*

(TANWEN is astonished by her own injury. 1st RP indicates her injury:)

Not true.
(1st RP crosses to LOWRI, strikes her again: points into TANWEN's face, cancelling their existence:)

Not true.
(TANWEN slumps. RPs look around. Then into audience.)

N7:

(JOE has suffered a stroke, has to be fed by BETI, who is partially sighted, almost blind.)

BETI: Hold on. Hold on. (*It is laborious*)

(JOE refuses, sated and/or tired.)

You need to have this. (*Renewed initiatives by both, till JOE spits out food.)*

(BETI throws down spoon.)

I CAN'T BEAR THIS.

I - CAN'T BEAR THIS.

I CAN'T BEAR - THIS.

(Pause)

You know I'm…

(Pause)

But

I can't

I CAN'T BEAR – THIS.

(They gaze at each other, until either BETI or JOE breaks the gaze.)

N8:

(Interrogation Room, where RONAN is in charge, in his professional capacity. TANWEN is bound, in a chair.)

TANWEN: Better than this.

RONAN: Not true.
You – shall let them down.
You're making me do this.

TANWEN: Hold on.

RONAN: I do what I must do.

TANWEN: Where's - ? *('LOWRI')*

RONAN: Oh, her? She kept banging on.
About taking off masks.
So we took hers off. And then, she broke. *(Shows TANWEN a photo. TANWEN gasps)*.
You.
You, won't make the same mistake.

TANWEN: (*wails for her dead lover, despairing*)
I can't bear this.

RONAN: *(objectively scientific)* Not true.
(hurts TANWEN)
You shall tell us, where to find the others.
You shall – let them down. You won't be sorry.
This is the beginning, of the end. Isn't it?
(hurts TANWEN)
I can take, all the time in the world. From you.

TANWEN: *(Sobbing)* I've lost my face.
(Gathers self) You're making me do this.
You're making me.

RONAN: *(sighs)* Keep you alive, till morning.
You'll be sorry.
You're making me do this.
(Steps in to start a new initiative on TANWEN.)

N9:

(In scene transition, as TANWEN and chair disappear, we see RONAN discard gloves, and don a jacket. RONAN is now in a semi-public place, such as a park, with AISLING. Sexual electricity crackles between them.)

AISLING: Hold on. We can take OUR time.
We can take all the time.
In the world.

RONAN: Now?

AISLING: You won't be sorry.

RONAN: *(Pause)* I won't –
Make the same mistake.

AISLING: You WON'T
Make the same mistake.
You're making me do – this – *(caressing foreplay)*

RONAN: (*Laughs, pleasurable outrage*) We can't.
(*RONAN looks around them.*) We CAN'T.

AISLING: Not true. Hey:
better than this:
hold on… *(AISLING goes further)*

RONAN: Ohhh – I can't bear this…

AISLING: You know I'm completely…?

RONAN: *(Looks around them again*) We CAN'T.
(Pause. Groans. Laughs.)

AISLING: We can't not. *(Light, whimsical provocation:)*
I shall – let them down.

RONAN: ??? Hold on. You can't –

AISLING: I can. I will. I shall.

RONAN: Ohhh. You know I'm completely…

AISLING: I know. (*whispers:*) I shall let them down.
(*AISLING reaches under her skirt to hitch down her pants, which fall to her ankles: gathers and discards them, deliberately.)*
You need to have this.

RONAN: *(Laughs)* I need to have this.

AISLING: *(Laughs.)*

N10:

(Back to Interrogation Room. TANWEN alone, still bound, broken in many ways.)

TANWEN: *(Pause)* I can't bear this. *(Pause)*

I shall let them down…

I SHALL let them down…

(Pause)

Hold on. I can't. This IS *(Pause)*

The beginning

Of

The end.

N11:

SION: (*tautstretched, frantic. Walks past CATRIN.*)
Hey. Hey.

CATRIN: Hey?

SION: You – (*SION proffers a neck chain he is wearing*)
Need to have this.

CATRIN: I …? Need…?

SION: NEED to have this.

CATRIN: (*reaches for the chain, SION withholds it:*
SION opens his palm). Not true.

SION: You NEED –

CATRIN: *(peers into* SION*; realizing, wary)*
You're making me do this.
(SION puts chain onto CATRIN. SION looks at CATRIN with doglike affection, admiration, dependency. SION extends palm.)

SION: You won't be sorry.

CATRIN: (*Gives money, but grabs and holds SION's wrist*)
YOU'RE. Making me do this.

(SION nods. CATRIN releases. SION runs off. CATRIN fingers the chain.)

N12:

(RONAN sits, listless: chronically depressed. AISLING enters, distracted.)

AISLING: (*seeking make-up)* I've lost my face.
(*Gazes at RONAN)*
Hey. *(Sympathetic*:) You have sad eyes.

RONAN: *(AISLING remains cheerful, applies make-up:*
knows she looks good.
Goes to RONAN. Looks concerned. Looks
grotesquely comical. Looks sexy. Looks curious.)

RONAN: It's never good enough. (*AISLING is nonplussed.)*
Nothing's any good. (*Pause)*

AISLING: You know I'm…

RONAN: Not true.

AISLING: ???
Hold on.

RONAN: We can't.
I can't bear this.

AISLING: You –

RONAN: Can't.

AISLING: *(Beat. Leaves. Returns with antidepressant medicine.)*
You
Need to have this.

RONAN: Not true. It's never good enough.
(Pause)
YOU'RE
Making me do
(gesture of disconnection)
This.

AISLING: ?
Not true.

RONAN: TRUE.

AISLING: *(Beat)* You have
SAD EYES!

RONAN: *(shrugs)* YOU
Have sad eyes.

AISLING: Not true. *(Beat)*

(She struggles inwardly.

She decides to exit, to fetch something.

She returns, holding something behind her back. She is struggling with her contending impulses, and near tears.)

Do you

NEED

To have

This?

(She offers him a pair of handcuffs. Beat.
She closes a cuff over one of her wrists,
and extends it to him.)

RONAN: (*looks into himself, then into her. Bluntly, but sadly:)*

It's never good enough.

AISLING: *(gasp-sobs: heartbroken.*

Then gradually summons and draws up her self-esteem.

She insists she is:)

Better than *(gesture to RONAN)*

THIS.

RONAN: Better than (*gesture to AISLING*)

THIS. (*AISLING gasps: with pain but also newly discovered anger.)*

AISLING: This

Is the beginning of the

END

Isn't it?

(Pause)

You're making me do

THIS *(gestures for RONAN to leave.)*

(RONAN does not leave. He stares back. Long pause.)

N13:

(JOE: & BETI)

BETI: *(Gesture:*
'I can't bear this').

JOE: *(Gesture:*
'I can't bear this').

BETI: *(Gesture:*
'You know I'm completely in love with you')

JOE: *(Gesture:*
'You know I'm completely in love with you')

BETI: *(Picks up pillow. Gesture:*
'You need to have this')

JOE: *(Gesture:*
'I need to have this'; 'You need to have this')

BETI: *(Gesture:*
'I can't')

JOE: *(Gesture:*
'Now')

BETI: *(Gesture:*
'You're making me do this')

JOE: *(Gesture:*
'You're making me do this')

BETI: *(Gesture:*
'We can't')

JOE: *(Gesture:*
'We can't not')('Better than this')
(BETI smothers JOE. It takes time. JOE is still.)
(BETI wails.)
(Slowly, she collects herself, and exits)
(Enter BONEBLACK. Studies JOE.)

BONEBLACK: *(discreet, precise, courteous, patient)*
Tell your story. *(Nods, thoughtfully.)*
Done:
army training:
teenage warfighting.
Known:
fear:
capture:
interrogation.
Done:
Defiance. Silence.
Known:

Loyalty. Death sentence. Terror.
Done:
Imagined firing squad. Bullets, aimed to tear precisely:
ripping through body, shredded while still awake,
still alive.
Then - ?
Known:
Armistice. Guards weep, as they surrender.
Shock at brutality of rescuers.
'Doing what they would have' - ?
Done:
Rampage. In prison camp: piss on desks and rugs.
In officers' quarters: swig four-star brandy.
Take to the road.
In haystack: sleep. In big house: shoot.
Break crockery. Slash paintings. Shit on carpet.
In next house: kill man. Take food. Fuck woman.
First time. Not good.
Take weapon, helmet, ammunition.
Known: release, from being human.
Release, from all things human.
Intolerable. But unforgettable. A second life.
Done:
Looting. Hiding. In small houses. No big houses.
He could have been them. Hate them for it.
They could have been him.
Fuck them for it.
Known:

Dysentery, sunburn, urge to sleep, urge to never stop, to rip and shatter everything, till it shines: and reflects.

Done:

Surrender.

Known:

Repatriation. Celebration. Third life.

Done:

Never tell. Work in factory.

Known:

Home. Wife. Child.

Done:

Never tell.

Known:

Fear. Courage. Madness. Boredom.

Done:

Hiding.

(A gesture: releasing JOE.)

Take it with you.

(BONEBLACK then takes in the audience:

shifts/cues the scene to...)

PART II: ALBEDO

Oliver Turner as Boneblack; Iona Greenslade as Annie.
Photos by Hubert Sikorski.

A1:

(..."UPSTAIRS":

not the contemporary human perspective. A gathering and convocation:)

RUBATO: The mayflies

BONEBLACK: They have their humanindicators:

RUBATO: Workeat fucksleep workdie
In their disconnection retention facilities:
Wallcaves
Insideout mirrorballs.

ANNIE: Some of them know: they've been sliced bitter.
They can't be anywhere, else. Anytime, else.
Didn't make the sea of shit,
where they or theirs float facedown.
Sadlake, of bodybloats and mindcrusts.
Otherfearfuls FLICT it on 'em, from
faroff or nextdoor.
All that effort, getting' born an' grown, an'
they never get to
(Beat)

BONEBLACK: Or even
(Beat)

M: Or even
(Pause)

RUBATO: Or even
(Pause)

RUBATO: Fortresses of worldfill
Barricaded anchortight. Lifeglue, steel
wombslammed against the wrongplace wrongface.
Whatfools: won't look beyond; and back.

ANNIE: We try to stop them rushing, with a stillpoint,
so they can smell it.

BONEBLACK: Some do.

ANNIE: Best use of a castle:
kiss in its ruins.
Spendwell, speedwell, dive in the pleasurewell.

RUBATO: But we can't make them.

BONEBLACK: So then:
WE'RE humanindicators.

(Double take by all:
reflecting on 'Who's in charge here?', Then:)

M: Notworth. Washouts. Cleanout and reset.
Time for whatsleft:
quieter, easier.

ANNIE: Mayflies aren't easy, not for long.

RUBATO: But nothing is.
That's why:
they MAY fly.
Timetake

BONEBLACK: Bestmake

ANNIE: Windsurge

BONEBLACK: Storm break. And then, break black.
As they must.

ANNIE: But they CAN:
nightconjure! And NOT die therefore.

M: Therefault:
theirfault. Landmining.

RUBATO: Hatching a countersun.

ANNIE: Shamewaste.

BONEBLACK: Trapmagnets.

RUBATO: Outscorching. Offshutting. Timeclosing.

M: So: nuffrope, willhang. Loosethefire!

ANNIE: NO. HEADLONG.

M: *(Spat with contempt)* 'Saviour'. Babymaker.

ANNIE: Handwasher. Mummifier.
Willhang, youwatch?

RUBATO: Holdback, leanback: stoprush.

ANNIE: STOPRUSH:
with a HEADLONG!

M: *(Spat with contempt)*
GloryBinder! Faultknot pre-tied.

BONEBLACK: Tidesin, tidesout.

ANNIE: Pointout ropecutter!

M: Backstepping…

RUBATO: Backstepping…

ANNIE: HandWIPING

M: LossCUTTING

ANNIE: Cuestranger. Rulechanger. Incoming!

M: "Mayflies": over and outclapped.
Checkmate!

ANNIE: PADLOCKER!
Checkmate, when you could let 'em fuckmate?

BONEBLACK: Outbursts.

ANNIE: Inroads!

RUBATO: Blowbacks.

ANNIE: Standaside. *('Action')*

RUBATO: Standaside. *('Inaction')*

BONEBLACK: Standaside. (*'Cautious hesitation'*)

M: Standaside. *('Counter-action: confrontation')*

(The tension tautens.)

(RUBATO and BONEBLACK turn away, leave. Then: M starts a new initiative, thinking he is alone. But ANNIE lingers, semi-hidden, watching. WEARHEAD is identified, from amongst the audience.)

A2:

M: Disaster?

WEARHEAD: Cities flood. Forests burn.
You just have to sense what's coming.
Be decisive.
Make it be: what it's gonna be.
Make things happen.
Roll with it. That's natural.
Every scarcity, every emergency,
provides an opportunity.
To put things in place. To put people in places.

M: Squalor?

WEARHEAD: I just know. My kids are worth more.
I am worth more. Than them.

M: War?

WEARHEAD: Peace won't buy or train the security forces.
Those guys are needed.
They have to patrol the gates.
I need to keep my kids safe.

M: Instinct?

WEARHEAD: I listen to what makes me feel right.
I trust my gut. Nothing else. No one else.

M: No one?

WEARHEAD: Not even my kids.
They've got their own priorities.
But I have to steer this thing, by mine.

M: Steer?

WEARHEAD: Maintain course.
Put the fear of God into those who won't.
Ask how they plan to feed their kids.

M: Kids?

WEARHEAD: There's kids, and kids.

M: Fear?

WEARHEAD: You have to let me do what I want.
Else: we can stop your kids being able
to do what they want.
Skin 'em, for their own good.

M: Slavery?

WEARHEAD: You gotta *earn* a living.
For those who'll work hard,
and need less sleep, we keep a ledge.
It's only slavery, if people know of something else.
If it's all you know: there's nothing
you can't get used to.
When something's happened, it's proved possible.
If it's possible, then it has to be acceptable.

M: Future?

WEARHEAD: I'll be long gone. New worlds to conquer!

M: Take me with you.

WEARHEAD: You're a shrewd judge of character, Mister - ?

M: Time I had a new name.
When Arthur had me made: my name was Mordred.
But I've had other names:
Manus, Woland, Abeminoth, Me-
(stops before saying 'Mephistophilis').
It's time I had a new one. Basically:
I'm here to offer you power.
Power like a pride, of many raging lions.
So why don't YOU call me:
'Manylion' *(pronounced 'Man- UL -ion').*
Bargain? *(Offers hand)*

WEARHEAD: I'm listening.

M: Deal. *(Clasps WEARHEAD's arm).*

This is the tumour.

(An effect of something striking WEARHEAD like a thunderbolt.)

Pass it around, before it wears you down.

Now you know your time is short,

you have to make the most of it.

Life isn't everything. So get what you can.

Seconds out.

(M vanishes. WEARHEAD leaves. ANNIE emerges, with BONEBLACK.)

A3:

ANNIE: Manylion keeps going downstairs.
Tinkering. Wankering.

BONEBLACK: It's what he does.

ANNIE: I know. Timenarrowing.
Seekin' out the other dominators.
Stokin' 'em up. Till they kill for possession.

BONEBLACK: They all have their stories. Peas in a pod.

ANNIE: Yeh, but. Unripe.

BONEBLACK: They all get time. They make it THEIR time.
Stretchedout joyous, stretchedout awful.
Cutshort brilliant, cutshort horrib*[le]* –

ANNIE: Yeh, but. When someone else, does
the stretchin' an' cuttin': there's no choice.

BONEBLACK: Often less. Than they think.

ANNIE: Yeh, but. MORE than they think.
(Beat) Manylion: he lets them down.

He's sellin' accumulation.
As if accumulation... (*Dawn of impulse:*)
Hey, Boneblack! I'LL make the time.
I'll go downstairs. If he can: I can!

BONEBLACK: You shouldn't do that.

ANNIE: I can't NOT.

BONEBLACK: ANNIE: YOU: shall let them down.
The mayflies.
Because you can't stay down there.
You might – upset the balance.
We have to acknowledge, that those things
– those creatures – are beyond our control.
And that is proper.

ANNIE: This ain't control. I don't do control.

BONEBLACK: We've noticed.

ANNIE: I wanna WEAN 'em OFF control.

BONEBLACK: *(indicating audience)* They're not your pets.
They're not your dolls.
And even you: can't be everywhere, all the time.
And that's just as well! *(Shudders)*
Think of the noise. And the mess!

Sometimes: bad decisions: make good stories.
So it's best not: to make them dependent.
Best not: to let yourself get INVOLVED.

ANNIE: But that's YOUR job.
You just observe, record and tidy them away.
I gotta have somethin' ter do, as well.

BONEBLACK: Well - I often think, I could do with a helper.
Literally, forever: rushed off my feet.
Lately, it's like being strapped to a treadmill,
then pushed down a helter-skelter.

ANNIE: Yeh, well. Boneblack: d'you ever think Manylion
is making YOU HIS helper?
What if: THEY forget US? Do WE die?
Look: what's the best thing about them?

BONEBLACK: (*Peers into audience.*
A pause, of some deliberation)
Some of them: can JUGGLE.

ANNIE: NO.

BONEBLACK: Some of them: learn how to KNIT.

ANNIE: NO. Some of them: CONNECT.
In the time available.

Even when everything is pushing them towards
disconnection: in their rules, in their system.
And that's the way that Manylion
is pushing them. Into fear.

BONEBLACK: His choice of work.

ANNIE: But why: should we let him have it all, his
way? Like they say downstairs,
'I don't trust him, any further
than I could throw a whisk'.

BONEBLACK: *(Double-take)* Who EVER said that?

ANNIE: If he's pushin' everythin',
an' everyone in his direction,
just to try to prove his point,
are we supposed to let him,
go along with that, all the way?
We didn't sign no treaty.
He just acts like we did, by dictatin' the pace.

BONEBLACK: Hold on –

ANNIE: YOU hold on.
If he's pushin' everything in one direction –
it NEEDS us, to push back, in the other.

BONEBLACK: WHAT does?

ANNIE: LIFE does.
Juss cos YOU spend all YOUR time planin' off
the edges, sweepin' up the shavings,
when the mayflies die, that don't mean we ALL
haveta take our eyes off what happens beforehand,
and it don't mean we can't make it
(grins) SURPRISIN'!
An' the best way t'start bein' surprisin', downstairs,
is to SHOW UP an' CONNECT,
an' start TWIZZLIN' THEIR WIGS!
HEYYY UP! INCOMING!!

BONEBLACK: Annie, now you are being as appallingly mad,
as a cat of bags.

ANNIE: *(Beat)* Don't you mean: mad as a bag of cats?

BONEBLACK: You: have evidently never: had to deal with
(intake of breath) a CAT of BAGS. *(shudders)*
I have.

ANNIE: Boneblack, it will be chaos forged with care.
Holistic havoc. And this time, I'll start off by
speaking the native language,
of wherever it is I touch down; because, usually,
that saves time *(she grins artfully, evidently*

thinking of an occasion when it didn't).

You can tell the others.

I'm off to show Manylion: he can't win.

I burst in every time.

An' start pissin' on his summer lawns.

(An effect of fire, air, transportation)

INCOMING!

With a mighty pudendous WHAMBUSH!!

AIR BORNE!!! *(she is gone)*

BONEBLACK: May the road rise with you. *(Beat)*

Peter fucking Pan.

A4:

("DOWNSTAIRS": the contemporary human perspective. M watches over SION & RONAN: they are apart, realities unshared)

M: You can't bear this.
You want to leave them behind.
You want to have your last word.
You want deliverance.
I'm here to tell you:
it's all yours.
(M gestures or clicks fingers:
SION and RONAN approach and enter their deaths:
SION takes an overdose,
RONAN commits suicide.)

M: Unfortunately, that doesn't mean you stop screaming.
But it does mean, that only I can hear you.
Fortunately, it's a sound that I've grown used to.
And there's no limit, to what you can get used to.
(He lingers and watches as:)
(CATRIN approaches the body of SION.
CATRIN checks for a pulse, finds none; fingers the chain round her neck, and starts to shake; takes out mobile phone, but finds all she can do is

scream into it; runs out.)

(AISLING approaches the body of RONAN.

Fights down her feelings, and stomach contents.)

AISLING: *(to audience)* Yes, I can identify.

That's him. *(Retches and vomits)*

(The trauma lets in disease: with which M strikes her like a thunderbolt. Slowly, laboriously, she walks off, under its weight.)

(Enter BONEBLACK. Goes to SION.)

BONEBLACK: *(discreet, precise, courteous, patient)*

Tell your story. *(Studies him. Nods, thoughtfully.)*

Done:

Consistently promising work at school.

Known:

carefree times:

strolling, by the canal.

Done: zero hour contract employment.

Slept through alarm. Missed a shift.

Known:

Unemployment. Disgrace.

Done:

rough sleeping.

Known:

Disappointment, with every thing.

Done:

heroin.

Known:

A lifting, of the pressure.

(A gesture: releasing SION.)

Take it with you.

(*Goes to RONAN.*)

BONEBLACK: *(discreet, precise, courteous, patient)*

Tell your story. *(Nods, thoughtfully.)*

Done:

Harm.

Known:

Love.

(A gesture: releasing RONAN)

Take it with you.

(To audience:) It's non-stop, today.

Always is.

A5:

WEARHEAD: (*watching images of worldwide unrest on monitor screens*)
I don't like this.
Isn't everything happening too fast?

M: We're just speeding up the process.
Starting its final stages.

WEARHEAD: But how much of that – will I get to see?

M: Well, nobody can see everything.
That's life! Or so I'm told.
Don't you all want to do something,
that ensures that nothing is quite the same,
ever again?
Leave a tear, shaped like you, in the fabric?
So you aren't forgotten?
You start the countdown.
I'm just oiling the wheels.

WEARHEAD: My kids are sick. They don't speak to me.

M: Just as well, that you can afford the best doctors.
Those who can't, more fool them.

WEARHEAD: People are rioting.

M: Good.
What you do next, is start a civil war in every country.
And you sell arms, profitably, to the side that will win.

WEARHEAD: But how will I know, which side will win?

M: It'll be the side with the most money, of course!
Do keep up.
Then you just gather resources
in tightly designated areas,
and make the rest uninhabitable.
It's like raising the rents in the cheaper side of the
city, so you get rid of the undesirable elements.
But on a global scale!
All life-supporting resources become merchandise,
of which you control the flow and function,
in terms of speculation and supply.
Amplify anxiety, and increase submission,
by implementing a subscription pricing model:
you change all products into services.
Which everyone has to be able to afford.
Who needs workers, when you can have slaves?
The quicker you move on this, the better.
It's basically a game,
but a game needs to have winners.

Just make sure that the ones,
who you have alongside you,
in the fortified central zone,
are the ones you can trust the most.
And you make sure of this by making them
even more scared, than those left outside!
Threaten those closest to you regularly:
in order to make sure they stay
the closest to you.

WEARHEAD: What are you getting out of this?
What's your incentive?

M: I'm just representing a clean, simple principle.
An element. The wind and the rain do what they
do: you decide who gets the shelter and the
housing. The wind and rain couldn't care less.
Say there's the image of a scary face.
It's the kids who decide when and where to use
it, to dare and to terrorize each other.
The image doesn't know, or care,
where it's inflicted. Neither do I.
That's my element: infliction.
Civilization couldn't function without me.

A6:

(A waiting room)

AISLING: I have a disease. And it's probably fatal.

DYFRIG: *(nods sympathetically)* My partner has a disease.
And it's probably fatal. *(Pause)*

AISLING: Well, they say we're all, just chemical reactions.
To the world around us. And what's happened.

DYFRIG: Yes. They say that. *(Pause.)*
But that doesn't really work, does it?
It's not like, another chemical reaction is going to,
come along, and take the place, of my partner.
Not for me, anyway. Nor for her, either. Nor for you.

AISLING: Well, I guess I won't know. Or care. I mean:
I didn't care about what was going on,
before I was born.

DYFRIG: No. Nor me. World War One passed us by.
Raged on without us. Just as well, really.

AISLING: Yes. Can't see how I'd have enjoyed any of that.
Though, apparently, some people did.

DYFRIG: Depending on, where they were, I suppose.

AISLING: Yes.

DYFRIG: I'm glad I'm here, now.

AISLING: I'm not sure. That I am.

DYFRIG: Well, it's awful sometimes. Of course. *(Pause)*
But then I think: it's a good thing,
that I told her how I felt, that day.
Because it meant:
we've had some wonderful times together.
Even now.
Everything's sharper and brighter.
And more important.

AISLING: *(Beat.)* Good.

DYFRIG: But now. We're waiting to hear,
from the consultant. *(Pause)*

AISLING: I didn't have enough, good times with my partner.
And very soon, I'm not going to be here, at all.
With anyone. For anyone. *(Beat.)*
Maybe - I'll be well out of it.
The future isn't looking - too good.

DYFRIG: True. There could be dark times ahead.
For all of us.

AISLING: *(strenuous cheerfulness)* Well, maybe not for me!
Less years of –
Pain and age and helplessness…
(realizes she is not exactly lightening the mood)
I mean, it all happens, but faster, but –
(realizes she is digging herself deeper into a hole)
You don't have to dwell on it. *(A gesture)* In it.

DYFRIG: No. You don't. *(A silence)*
But I want to. Dwell in it.
I want her to dwell in it. While we can.
Because it's going to end.

AISLING: I don't like this life. I don't like the hand,
I've been dealt.
My partner, he left this tear in the fabric.
And it keeps mocking me.
Because I can't reach him anymore.
To argue back, or make him listen.
And have my say.
And make HIM sorry.
He's placed himself beyond me.
But I can't get myself – beyond him.
You see, the problem is, I loved him.
But it wasn't enough. Evidently.

To stop him – hating being alive.
And I can't bear that.

DYFRIG: (*doing his desperate best*)
Do you have any hobbies?

A7:

(CATRIN is working in a care home. BETI is a patient. CATRIN offers BETI medication. BETI shuns it, naughtily. CATRIN persists.)

BETI: Life isn't. Going to get. Any better for me.
In here. Is it?
I could. Take those pills. And go down. Into mush.
Not death. Just mush.
So I'm. Barely aware. That it's someone. Else.
Who's having. To deal.
(to CATRIN, with consciously wicked intent)
With my bowel movements. And bedsores.
Because they will. Have to.
When. Those pills. Turn me. Into mush.
Why. Are you. Working here. Amongst the mush?
Helping. To make us. Even mushier?

CATRIN: I'm trying to do, something good.

BETI: What?

CATRIN: It helps me – to feel better about myself.

BETI: Watching me. On the slow drag down. Makes you.
Feel better. About yourself?

CATRIN: No. Yes.

BETI: You've a sick. Taste. In spectator. Sports. *(Beat)*

CATRIN: Look: you evidently don't have any family left.
(Her tolerance snaps)
Who can BEAR to deal with YOU!
Anymore. That's why you're here.
That's why you're all here. It gives you dignity.
While you wait. *(Pause)*

BETI: Call this. Dignity? I call it. Being pumped full.
Of cotton wool.
So that nothing. Matters.
I think. You're wasting. Your time.
I don't. Really mean. Anything. To you.
So I. Don't matter. To you.
Neither. Do they.
You're trying. To make things. Not matter.
To you. So that everything's. Non-stick.
(with baleful glee) But you can't.

CATRIN: No, I'm trying to make a difference.
By being good. On a small, daily basis.

BETI: No, you're stuck. In yourself. Just like we are.
Glued up. With care. It's all. That's keeping.
You. Together. 'Cept. It's not.

CATRIN: I'm looking after people who can't
look after themselves, any more.
So that they aren't having to sit around,
in their own shit.

BETI: While they wait.

CATRIN: Yes.

BETI: Wait. For what? *(Pause)*

CATRIN: Some of these people, have had very sad lives.
And some would be in terrible pain.
Now they're glad of the relief. *(Pause)*
I'm trying to be kind.

BETI: Oh, for God's sake. Woman.
Get me. Out of here.
And take me. Somewhere. Where I can get.
A DECENT SHERRY. *(Venomously)*
Else I'll. Come back. And haunt you.

A8:

(TANWEN: out on the street: released from prison, disfigured; looks around, breathes in the isolation.)

TANWEN: I've nothing.
I'm nothing. Not any more, without you.
There's nothing I can do, or say.
Nothing left. Not any more.
So I won't kid myself. It's all over.
(An effect of air and fire: ANNIE materializes)

ANNIE: *(oppressively hyper-enthusiastic)* SHMAE, CONT!

TANWEN: *(disbelieving, uncomprehending, agog)*

ANNIE: *(nods)* Rhyfeddol? Ie? ANHREFN DWI!
Mae rhai yn fy ngalw'n ANNIBENDOD.
Ond mae ANNIE'n iawn. Cytuno, Dolores?
(Stepping over into Downstairs.)
Bendigeid –
(spreads her arms like the wings of a crow)
FRÂÂÂN! *(Looks around)* BENDIGEDIG!
(Snap Blackout. Interval.)

PART III: CITRINAS

Matthew Sole as Rubato; Iona Greenslade as Annie.
Photos by Hubert Sikorski.

C1:

TANWEN: What the FUCK are you on about?

ANNIE: Fi jyst wedi meddwl – 'dy ni ddim yn mynd
i ddatrys y problemau, os ydym yn siarad
yn yr iaith a achosodd y problemau. Sori!
(does something to trigger translation)
I just thought: we ain't gonna SOLVE
the problems, by talkin' in the language
that CAUSED the problems.

TANWEN: I only speak English.

ANNIE: You can change that, pilgrim.
'And the wise man said: Free your mind
and your ass will follow'.
Or maybe: the ass knows it's Palm Sunday:
and it says 'I'll let YOU go FIRST'! *(Beat)*
If you see a brown patch on me, it's a dead moth.

TANWEN: Who the fuck ARE you?

ANNIE: I am ANHREFN! *(Strikes a pose, then drops it:)*
But you can call me ANNIE.

ANNIE dranginastürm, ANNIE roadup,
Miss Rule, Polly Amorous
(winks at TANWEN, and also an audience member).
Meddwl amdanaf fel rhyw fath o –
Twm Sion Catwoman!
(*TANWEN looks nonplussed*).
Sdim ots. I'm here to twizzle your wig, but in a
sly, gentle, arousing sort of way.
You WILL thank me for it. Through your tears.

TANWEN: Why me?

ANNIE: Things happen quicker: for those with less to lose.
They've less fear.
I'm gonna Easter Egg you Onwards.
Then YOU: will do what you mayflies do best.
Which is make some events an' memories:
for yourself; an' for the other mayflies.
Think of it, like this: you've taken this bus ride,
every day, but you've never been up on the top deck.
Cos you never knew, that the bus was A DOUBLE
DECKER. Till NOW. You'll be amazed.
At what you can see! Down AN' into!

TANWEN: Look. If you're pushin': I'm stayin' off the drugs.

ANNIE: I'm only pushin' YOU, pilgrim. Pushin' you ON.

TANWEN: Are you some sorta – personal trainer?

ANNIE: (*in sudden bizarre Black Country accent*)
In a manna uv spaykin' (*And out of it. Grins*).
Look: I'm just comin' straight
outta my own nonsense. Like we all are.
But I'll try an' give you the overview:
in just the three dimensional slices,
that you can currently fathom.
A few Bertolt Brechdannau.
(*Beat. TANWEN looks blank. ANNIE conjures*
a plot summary so far: a narrative-process that
progresses from the simple to the wonderful to
the horrifying to the completely discombobulating.
TANWEN is completely discombobulated).

ANNIE: I can see, how all this might come as a
bit of a shock, to try an' get your head round.

TANWEN:

ANNIE: I know, why don't you take a shot of this,
to sort you out.
(Produces a hipflask, offers it to TANWEN,
who takes several gulps) But go steady.

TANWEN: !!!

ANNIE: Strong stuff, innit?
I remember givin' some o'this to that poet,
Percy Shelley, when everythin' I said made him
a bit - banjaxed.
Percy was a nice bloke, but 'e WAS a bit deaf.
So he says t' me, 'Fuck me, what d'you call
THIS?' I says, I call this The Flask of Anarchy.
He says, 'Hell's TEETH, if I can't write a fuckin'
poem, on the back of the buzz off THAT,
I might as well HANG MY OWN COCK'.
Good job for him, an' for Mary, that he didn't.
Now listen: you need to get yourself a squad.
A Firm. So what you do, is: you trawl the bars.
The parks. The libraries.
You round up, some of the hopeless.
You spread the word.

TANWEN: What word?

ANNIE: You ease them together, through the only thing
that they will have in common:
the cascading currency of DESPERATION!
And I will arrange for you: a visit.
A Session with Rubato.

TANWEN: What's Rubato? A person? Or a thing?

ANNIE *(nods)* Exactly! Rubato: is The Genius, of Time.

He can appear briefly, in human form.
Well, what looks like it. Almost.
And he gives, you and them: The Word.

TANWEN: O-kay…

ANNIE: It will be titanic. A gathering of counterforces!

TANWEN: I'll – make a start...

C2:

(BETI, DYFRIG, AISLING, CATRIN assemble, in a meeting room, sizing each other up. ANNIE enters, scrutinizes them, with some distaste. ANNIE is invisible to them. TANWEN enters.)

ANNIE: Are you havin' a LAUGH? THIS LOT?
This is the BEST you could DO? Or find?

TANWEN: No. Yes. Well, like I said - it's a START.

ANNIE: THIS LOT?
THIS is the crack squad, which you have summoned?
This is who you reckon you can work with,
strategically, to lever up the whole HINGE,
of human history an' consequence?
WYRD sense o' humour, pilgrim. Call this a FIRM?
Looks ter me more like a LIMP!

TANWEN: Thank you all. For coming. For this meeting:
I've managed to arrange for you – something special.
A rare visit, from someone very important.
(A ripple of uneasy anticipation. RUBATO appears.)

RUBATO: I have to point out now: that I don't have all day.

TANWEN: We're all very grateful. For your presence.

RUBATO: So Anhref – so Tanwen here –
has arranged for me to speak to you,
individually and together.
She seems to think it might do some good.
(Scans those assembled) Fuck knows why.

TANWEN: We are grateful for your time.

RUBATO: Yeah, well. Everyone says that time is marvellous.
And necessary! But no one can agree:
on WHAT it IS.
It pisses me off.
(Pause. Some shifting about.)

AISLING: Time has become - particularly precious to me.
You see:
I have this disease. And I haven't –

RUBATO: Shut up. You've had more time, than many.
Who've had worse times.
(Awkward pause. AISLING sinks back down, bemused.)

BETI: I find. I don't know what. To do. With myself.
Since my husband died. I don't. Go out anymore –

RUBATO: Shut up! So: why should anyone,
give a damn about you?
If they never see you? And you don't see anyone?

BETI: I can't help it. That I can't. See anyone! I'm blind –

RUBATO: Shut up! So: learn an instrument.

BETI: But that! Will take! Ages! –

RUBATO: So: wake up earlier! And stay up later. Next!

DYFRIG: I'm waiting, to hear back from the hospital, about my –

RUBATO: Shut up. There's a song: *(sings, alarmingly)*
'To wait for love /Is just to wait your life away'.
She *(BETI)* can learn to play it. On the instrument.
That she's GOING *(glaring intently at BETI)* to
learn. And she can play it: AT YOU.
Till you GET A LIFE. BACK! Next!

CATRIN: I still - can't forgive myself - for what I did, when I –

RUBATO: Shut up! What were you?
Bitten by a radioactive sock puppet?
Chuck away whatever it is, that's got its hand up you,
and is speaking through your mouth.
AND chuck away whatever YOU are,

letting it have its way. It's the least you owe yourself. Show it, who's in charge here. Next!

TANWEN: I've nothing.
I'm nothing. Not any more, without her.
There's nothing I can do, or say.
Nothing left. Not any more.
So I won't kid myself.
It's all – *(ANNIE is increasingly exasperated with TANWEN)*

RUBATO: Oh, shut up.
We've all heard you, go through all that DRIVEL, in the first part: before the interval.
(THE FIRM are puzzled by this comment).
In future: never say anything twice.
For as long as you live.
That's one step towards making you bearable.
(Beat) You sought out conflict. You knew the risk. So did she.
If what you did scared them,
because they were unjust, then call them to account. And scare them some more.
Right. Let me talk you through what I call:
The Gospel of Good Riddance.
(Pause. ANNIE responds as if her favourite band has announced her favourite song!)
So, for starters: You all clamber over yourselves.

An' you tell your selves: to fuck off.
'Cos at the moment: you lot contain,
all the presence an' charisma:
of five over-stuffed black plastic sacks.
WAITING to be slung on The Dustcart of Despair.
You desperately want to be loved, but you're not.
COURSE YOU'RE NOT.
WHAT'S LOVEABLE ABOUT YOU?
Right now: you're not really interested, in being loved.
Because you don't think it's realistic:
for anyone to love you.
COURSE IT ISN'T. BUT SO WHAT?
Fuck realism.
If realism were true, we'd never get anything done.

TANWEN: *(raises her hand, starts to speak)*
I think I have to tell you, this makes me feel –

RUBATO: Spare me this endless rambling self-description!
You're all CLINGING onto betrayal.
Like it was a PINK RUBBER DINGHY!
NEWS FLASH:
It's THE SHARK!

BETI: A shark? Where? I can't see –

CATRIN: Don't panic! It's not a REAL SHARK!

RUBATO: AHA! YOU SAY that!
But are YOU a REAL PERSON - ?

CATRIN: Of course I'm a real person,
how dare you come – *('in here and...')*

RUBATO: YET? Break the habit of a lifetime. Entertain a possibility. Work your experience. Explore consequence. Ditch The Shame. Don't hug it like a blanket! Chuck The Grief.
Don't suck it like a dummy, yum yum -
WHAT D'YA THINK GRIEF IS? TREACLE?
Transformation will require you to SWEAT
And to PANT, till your snatched breath
starts to turn you into someone else entirely.
And not a moment too soon.
Peel off the old self, pull on a new one.
Takes a bit of work.
But what d'ya think life is, a FREE GIFT?
What d'ya think you are, ENTITLED to it?
(Beat.) Someone out there is deciding,
FOR you, what is real.
What could be real. What should be real. *(Beat.)*
But. On whose terms? In whose interests?
As, I gather, you say round here:
Cloddia.
(Pause)

And:

When you've no time to waste,

you slow down, an' slide, through the gaps,

between the moments. *(Beat)*

You're welcome.

I have to run. Out.

(He is gone)

ANNIE: (*very pleased with herself*)

HOW about THAT, then?

TANWEN: *(less sure of herself)* How about that, then?

(The humans glance at each other shiftily, in clammy silence.)

C3:

(CATRIN & AISLING together. ANNIE watches. TANWEN, walks past, pauses, intrigued by their body language, to watch unseen)

CATRIN: You know:
I really like your name. I've not heard it before.
It makes me think of, a pool of rain
With a tree, to one side;
And this tree has things, hung in its branches,
That chime, in the breeze.
Plus: you have a really great nose.

AISLING: Well - I really like your nose.
And your name
And your look.
They suit.
You look sort of –
like a cat that's been sewn up in a woman's skin
And it's struggling to get out.
But in a good way.
I like that. *(Beat.)*
Pity I'll be dead soon.
(Pause. Their lips become magnets,
drawing them into a kiss.)

CATRIN: Meeeeeyyyyowwww. *(Beat)* Well, let me tell you.
You: are not dead yet.
(They slink off, together, louchely.)

TANWEN: Annie! Can't you – do something, for Aisling?
Can't you – make her well?

ANNIE: I keep tellin' you mayflies, I can't start tinkerin'.
I can only make suggestions. Nindicate.

TANWEN: An' that's the best I've ever seen Catrin.
It seems such as waste, if they can't…

ANNIE: Well, look. There is somethin', YOU could try.
But it carries risks: for YOU.
You look Aisling deep in the eyes:
then you put your hand on her back:
then you breathe into the tumour,
that's inside her; an' you try to suck it out.
Some of you mayflies are able to do that.
But you don't know it. So you don't try it.
Maybe: you're one of those, who can.
It's worth a shot.

TANWEN: Right. Okay!
So what's the risk?

ANNIE: You draw it out of her: an' you draw it into yourself. But. If you can't breathe it out, you could be, stuck with it.
(Pause)

TANWEN: I'll try it. Aisling! C'mere a minute.
(Pause) Aisling!
It's important! *(Pause)* Aisling,
you need to come here
NOW!

AISLING *(rearranging herself)*:
Your fucking timing. It's impeccable.
What is it, that can't wait?
(TANWEN holds her, looks into her: it is strangely intimate: she turns AISLING, places her hands on her back, breathes out and in, out and IN:)
(It is as if AISLING feels something lift out of her. And TANWEN senses something previously unknown. Pause.)

TANWEN: I think – you ought to – arrange a check-up.
An update.

AISLING: I might. I've also been thinking:
maybe I don't want to know.
Any more.
But that felt strange. Thank you.
(Pause. AISLING exits.)

ANNIE: Tanwen. I think YOU.
Should – get yourself checked out.
In case, you didn't –

TANWEN: Maybe *I* don't want to know.
(Pause) (Enter DYFRIG)

DYFRIG: I saw that. I saw what you did. To her. Why?

TANWEN: ?

DYFRIG: Why didn't you offer to do that: to MY WIFE?
I can't believe it. I can't believe you didn't ask me.
Her.
Do it again! To her! Now!
(TANWEN is lost for words)
You won't?
(TANWEN, drained, makes a gesture of emptiness.)
I will never forgive you for that!
I wish YOU were the one who was dying!
That was UNFORGIVABLE! *(He goes)*
*(TANWEN stares, unfocussed.
ANNIE places her hand on TANWEN's shoulder.
TANWEN shrugs it off, and exits.)*

C4:

(BETI is practicing the violin. Appallingly.
DYFRIG enters, listens for as long as he can bear.
He is desperate to talk to someone, anyone. At last:)

DYFRIG: Can you just - stop that for a moment? Please?
(She does.)
How did you manage? When your husband died?
How did you cope?
You see, my wife's in hospital,
and she could go at any minute now.
And I want to be with her.
But I can't bear being in the hospital, any more.
And I don't think, she can tell that I'm there.
Despite what they say.
And I can't do anything, there. Except sit.
And look at her.
That's not – how I want to be with her.
When she dies, I want to die, as well.
Did you feel like that? *(Beat)*

BETI: Not really.

DYFRIG: Why not?

BETI: I wanted to see. What it was like. Without him.

DYFRIG: What was it like?

BETI: Better. And worse. *(Beat)*

DYFRIG: But you carried on. You carry on.
You're even – learning – to play – the bloody violin.

BETI: Yes.

DYFRIG: Why?

BETI: I don't know. Really. *(Beat)*
(Enter AISLING, ecstatic. She has heard she's been cured, AND she's in love. She moves quickly across the stage, hugging herself, saying:)

AISLING: Oh. My. God. Oh my GOD. Oh MY GOD.
OH mygod, OH mygod.
OMIGOD OMIGOD OMIGOD
OMIGOD OMIGOD OMIGOD -
(AISLING is gone)

DYFRIG: What was all that - ?

BETI: Low Flying. Atheist. *(Beat)*

DYFRIG: I heard Tanwen, talking to herself again.
With those voices: she says she hears. *(Beat)*

Like Joan of Arc.
That's it: she thinks she's Saint bloody Joan.
Not just a mad bloody witch. *(Beat)*
She did something, to try to help Aisling.
With her illness. And I hated her.
Because she didn't try it on Gwenllian.
Though it's probably too late, for Gwenllian.
From what they say, at the hospital.
Anyway. I said to Tanwen, I wished
she was the one, who was dying. *(Beat)*
I shouldn't have done that. *(Beat)*
I don't know what to do. Any more. *(Pause)*

BETI: Gwenllian. If you can find. A way to be with her.
After. Then you will.

DYFRIG: How?

BETI: I don't know. Really. But you will.
Sometimes. I think. There's no afterlife. *(Pause)*
But sometimes. I think. There might be.
And I think. What might be even worse.
Than no afterlife. Is that. There is one.
And you meet them. Again. Your husband.
Or your wife. And you know them. But they.
Don't know you. Any more.
And that's very. Peculiar. *(Pause)*

DYFRIG: So – what do you do? Then?

BETI: Well, you get over them.
And carry on. I suppose.
Or else. You start flirting. With them.
And with everybody else. That might be.
Quite good.

DYFRIG: Flirting? With EVERYBODY else? *(Beat)*
I feel tired, just - thinking about it.

BETI: Well. You're just tired, then. And so, you.
Will get a rest. *(Beat)*
But we've. Got some things.
We can do, first. Tanwen says.
So I like to hear. What she's got to say.
Or what she hears.
It might be right.

DYFRIG: Yes. It might. She might.

PART IV. RUBEDO

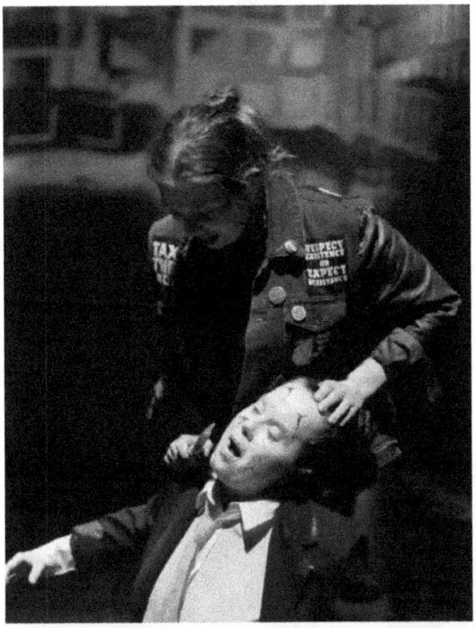

Jade Roberts as Wearhead, Katherine Taylor as Tanwen; Adrianna Wanda Czajczynska as Aisling, Rachel Barwise as Catrin. Photos by Hubert Sikorski.

R1:

ANNIE: Ready?

TANWEN: Guess so.

ANNIE: *(Briefly, into Black Country again)*
This will be BOSTIN' brilliant. *(and out)*
But it will have actual impact:
on the human world. *(and in)*
So that's why it needs one of YOW.
To set it up.

TANWEN: Right.
(ANNIE taps her translation unit,
clears her throat.)

ANNIE: You will create awaken and harness forces.
Which will create:
The Most Spectacular Event,
In The History Of The World!
Nothing less
While your team draw the fire –

TANWEN: O-kay –

ANNIE: It'll be kinda like the Bruce Lee tactic,
'Be Water, My Friend',
But in reverse!

TANWEN: Yeah. No. Yeah…

ANNIE: And You:
will let the Virus:
into the Fortress. So that the Future – unlocks!

TANWEN: ???

ANNIE: But to trigger this
You have to conjure
You have to wake up, and activate:
The Lynx of Meri Wells.

TANWEN: The what?

ANNIE: The Lynx of Meri Wells. *(Beat)*

TANWEN: What the fuck is that?

ANNIE: HE's - kind of like a Golem Ferryman
Statue Whisperer.
On ONE whole plain, of material reality.
An' sometimes, a bit of a Cosmic Banksy.

TANWEN: You been at that flask?

ANNIE: I know, you COULDN'T make it up.
'Less you were me. But you can only address
him, and request his abilities, once.
In the living memory, of everyone on Earth, at that
time. So you gotta make it count. Which you will.
Because you must.

TANWEN: So - what is it, we're gonna ask him to do? Exactly?

ANNIE: How shall I put this? *(Beat)*
He can dissolve the boundaries between the living
and the dead. Or, rather, statues. AND ceramics.

TANWEN: Statues?

ANNIE: AND ceramics. *(Pause)*

TANWEN: Wow. *(Beat)*
I did once knew someone, who had this –
morbid FEAR of statues. But that was one person.
She was a bit – atypical.
Even if this – Lynx? –
can make some things – move around a bit,
d'ya think that's really gonna make a difference?
'Unlock the future'?

ANNIE: I usually find, with the Lynx,
that it takes a minute or two.
To get him going.
But once he's away, he's very -
He is very. Just very.
And he is - thorough.

TANWEN: *(Hesitant)* All right…

(ANNIE and TANWEN prepare the space, and TANWEN, for an invocation. ANNIE does so in a way that is both (a) uncharacteristically scarily intent, and (b) daft.)

ANNIE: And now, you have to speak the words
on this paper. *(opens it for TANWEN)*

TANWEN: Bogadh na nDealbh.
(*pronounced 'Boga na Nee –yal – iv', keeping
the sound in the back and top of the mouth.*)
(*Pause.)* I don't think this is going to work.

ANNIE: Look. I can't do this for you.
Your existence is finite: VERY finite.
And you can count on nothing to protect you,
or evaluate you, or offer your life meaning.
Except yourself. Just sayin'.

TANWEN: Thanks. Loads.

ANNIE: So you're decidin' to spend these moments,
that are tickin' away, standin' there an' sayin'
'I don't think this is going to work'?
You just don't want to play, do you?
Well, pilgrim, it's the only game in town.
But it's your call. *(Beat)*
And right now, that's the problem, with you humans:
You ain't believin', the stories you're telling
yourselves. So make some new ones.

TANWEN: That's spiritsplaining. You're as bad as Rubato.

ANNIE: What have you got to lose?

TANWEN: *(Pause)* Bogadh na nDealbh.
(A whole side of reality dissolves.
THE LYNX is made manifest.)

THE LYNX: So The Lynx yawns. An' he stretches.
Guardian doorman at the portal of the possible.
Behind his shades:
The Eyes, once opened, never blink.
His branded shoulders LAUGH at self-preservation.
His scars say, 'Preserving the self?
Whadda ya think the self is? JAM?'

ANNIE: Actually. That's what Rubato said to Lynx.
The one time, Rubato caught him, having a whimper.

THE LYNX: DO YOU MIND?
I AM NOT 'LYNX'. I AM 'THE LYNX'.
Batman wouldn't introduce himself as
'Batman', would he?
He'd make DAMN sure everyone called him
'The Batman'!
And I have NEVER in my WHOLE
EXISTENCE "had a whimper". *(Snorts)*
NOW DO YOU WANT MY HELP, OR NOT?

TANWEN *(obeying ANNIE's gestures and grimaces of* insistence): Yes. Yes.

THE LYNX: It requires CONCENTRATION! *(Pause)*
Right. Where was I? If they're callin' on him,
somethin' is goin' down.
An' there's serious work to do.
So: like a calloused boulder:
The Lynx hunches down, into his justly
renowned an' legendary, laconic yet remorseless,
stance: ter FOCUS!

ANNIE: The main drawback with – The – Lynx: is that
he is – downright incessantly – self-dramatizing.

THE LYNX: Those scars say: stand back, folks.
Give The Lynx some space, an' time,
to load an' pump the bellows.

An' stretch a new horizon.
He starts to kindle the coldfire.
This stuff jumps, you can see his scorchmarks.
But he pays them no mind, no more than the welts
an' lashes on his back, from when he's had someone,
something, to shelter. From the hellburst.

ANNIE: But he's the one to do the job.

THE LYNX: So The Lynx gleans, he's gotta use what HE alone
KNOWS: t'summon the forces,
spark the friction, make that crackshot
deadeye penalty kick that will convert the fear
into ASTONISHMENT.

ANNIE: But he does go on a bit. You thought I was bad?

THE LYNX: And The Lynx feels his hackles rise.
His snout truffles THE AIR ITSELF!
His ears TWITCH!

ANNIE: But it seems to be what he needs,
to get himself into the zone. To get stuff done.

THE LYNX: He sends out The Call.
(Pause)
I said, he sends out THE CALL.
(Pause)

Gordon Bennett.
HE! SENDS OUT! THE CALL!
(Pause)
(Inspired) AND SURE ENOUGH!

TANWEN: I can't hear a damn thing.

ANNIE: Sshh.

THE LYNX: Things WILL rumble apart:
an' recombine.
Plates shift apart, an' start to spin.
Spreadin' the life around,
into cruel an' unusual forms an'
crannies, so the usual wings do not apply.
Jadies and lentilmen:
It's SHOW TIME!
It STARTS:
in a way both separate an' cataclysmic:
Silent figures appear on the tops of all city
buildings, worldwide. They gaze down.
Citizens stop an' gaze back up, at these blank
and brooding bodyforms, that resemble
Antony Gormley's cast iron shapes.
The citizens wonder: are these the heralds
of a mass headlong lemming suicide?
Or are they peerin' down and searchin' for
something, in the suddenly created and united

international legions of the gobsmacked?
It STARTS: in a way, both small an' huge:
In the northern Cymru market town of Corwen,
steam surges from the nostrils of a stone horse.
Its rider, Owain Glyndwr, twirls his sword.
The horse's eyes smoulder; he SNORTS,
tosses his mane an' rears up. Then both rider an'
steed bolt off down the high street, hwylin' away,
fillin' sails to astonish, an' pledging to puncture
the goblins of entitlement; or, as Owain shouts:
'MAE AMSER WEDI DOD, I DYLLI'R PWCI
RHYFYGUS!'
Sure enough: it all starts to LIFT OFF.
The Lynx busts some new kids out the kiln.
The stir their stumps, an' join the fray.
Leadin' the parade is Saint Bartholomew:
waving a banner of his skin he has peeled off
himself. He strides out, shouting an' singing loudly:
'What a wonderful day, ter
TURN YERSELF INSIDE OUT! WHEN
YOUR EYES NEED SOME REFRESHMENT,
DON'T JUST PEER DOWN AT YER PHONES!
'TAIN'T NO SIN, TER TAKE OFF YER SKIN!
AN' DANCE AROUND IN YER BONES!'
When people SEE him, they laugh hysterically,
faint at the sight, or do both in quick succession.
But he is just the overture to the Red. Raw. Meat.
Taking another cue from Damien Hirst,

The Lynx triggers a volcanic emergence from debris:
a ten-metre-high woman, half anatomized to reveal a pregnancy amongst her entrails.
She screws off her head, and uses it to smash down any abstract memorials to fallen soldiers.
She screams out: 'No COLUMNS, no GARLANDS!
Just THIS! and THIS!'
As she points to her own ragged neck.
And the orphaned stillborn baby in her gut.
From the obelisks and cenotaphs she has shattered,
rises a fleet of metallic winged figures, even bigger than Alfie Bradley's Knife Angel.
Each has a hollow in his chest: marking life unlived.
The semi-flayed woman sprouts wings, takes to the air,
swoops low over Coventry Cathedral and shouts out
'C'mon, Mickey, don't be SHY'.
In response, Jacob Epstein's St Michael cracks free of the cathedral frontage.
He embraces her in mid-air, kisses her boneflesh face,
and they FUCK, loudly and passionately.
Drenching those below!
Panicked governments mobilize armed forces against the worldwide eruptions of advancing winged colossi, a murmuration cyclone sprung from cemeteries
an' cathedrals like birds from cages.
But, wherever they do, the blade angels rear up out of nowhere, hoover up their hardware,
an' grow huger in the process.

The armies look on like furious crippled ants.
Try kettling THAT!
Military computers are stalled by the realization:
that The Unforeseeable is happening.
And it wears a cheeky grin, as it punches, with its full weight; and spreads out, worldwide.
In Detroit, the statue of Baphomet,
the Dark Lord of the Satanic Temple,
goes down on all fours, bleats like a goat an' starts playing with a ball of string.
Then he breaks into a ridiculous high-kicking jig, singing the tune of the stunningly banal 1960s hit single,
'The March of the Mods'. He announces
'I'm not The Devil, I'm just yer Uncle Mithras, come to celebrate the union of opposites! Satyr Day is here, hairy and winkin' atcha!
Let's get the Sex Magic Party STARTED!
Who's brought the mushrooms?'
Media commentators quickly identify this,
and similar global events, as hallucinations reflecting mass hysteria, triggered by the psychological insecurity, which has been caused by an unusual configuration of political, cultural and historical factors.
The Lynx chuckles, shrugs his shoulders an' says,
'That's just the way things go round here,
when push comes t'shove'.
Presidents and prime ministers order their military
to send in forces and issue an ultimatum.

Because that is what the military does.
The military promises ostentatious strength and
simultaneous lobotomization into inflexibility.
They won't permit themselves: to have a clue.
On the outskirts of Rome, the earth rumbles
round the Stadio dei Marmi: a 1920s sports complex,
designed for the Italian Fascist Academy of Physical
Education, and flanked by fifty-nine statues.
The stadium is now a training ground for young people
of mixed ethnicities; but the presiding statues are sternly
Aryan, brutalist and glowering.
Yet, when The Lynx breaks out his sticks and brings the pulse of sly beats: the statues start to tap their feet, roll their musclebound shoulders, shimmy their ample hips: letting their innate camp tendencies flourish. They clamber down from their pedestals and stride out away from the stadium, which now resembles a set of toothless gums. The Marmi Boys approach the city and zero in on the chants of a right-wing white-pride homophobic rally.
The statues encircle the startled fascists and herd them into a main road, where the traffic has to screech to a halt.
Then the Marmi Boys break into song: they regale the fascists with booming baritone renditions of 'I'm Coming Out', 'Sing If You're Glad to be Gay', 'I Am What I Am' and 'Dancing Queen'.
All the time, they exhort the fascists to embrace and brandish their most feared and denied impulses.
Under this sustained and unusual pressure, several do

indeed twitch, spasm, and snap: into what can only be described as a raging queerness; and they proceed to get down, deep into the groove: to the horror of their former colleagues.
The Lynx permits himself a dry chortle at this:
the same dry chortle that HE taught to Keith Richards.
Face it, kids: The Impossible is happening; and having
A Gathering: with STYLE! You just gotta learn to love it.
Inside the British House of Commons, the Right Honourable Member for Dessication-in-Wanking shakes his head and mutters that 'Disruptive forces are challenging our world'.
Damn right we are. On a mission: our purpose to overturn the dominant human terms of reality and consciousness.
An' we're just getting' started!
Reports are coming in of a new initiative, focussed on the West coast of Wales, in a town called Aberystwyth.
At the head of the town stand two statues by Mario Rutelli, embodying two forms of Victory.
Caught on camera, we see the upper wing woman breaking free from her perch, flying up to summon and lead the massed murmuration of blade angels, and repelling the converging patrols of military aircraft with an ear-splitting roar of 'DROS RHYDDID: NO PASARAN'.
Her proudly naked sister sends a pulse: down into the ocean bed. Beneath the crustacean bed, something is unmooring, and unfolding, with a seismic force…
Resounding across The Irish Sea: over which Winged Victory and her flock soar and swoop, belting out a raucous rendition of the song 'The Rocky Road to Dublin', until

they land in O'Connell Street. They are greeted and invited into uproarious stone shenanigans by Jim Larkin, Bernard Shaw and James Joyce. Oscar Wilde serves luminous green cocktails!
Phil Lynott steals a bass, plugs in, and
Molly Malone starts belting out
'The Girls are Back in Town'
[SFX: opening riff of this].
And the ocean pulse digs deeper, and the Irish Famine Statues creak, stir and flex...
preparing themselves for a crossing...
Back in the British Parliament, The Right Honourable Member for Dessication-in-Wanking is appealing to the enshrined values that have made this country what it is. Which The Lynx will translate for you, now, as: fear of youth, fear of time, fear of decline, fear of impotence, fear of insignificance, fear of difference, fear of each other.
Right on cue: clambering up out the Thames, a set of babylonishly daubed mad and mangy lions!
Which The Lynx has quickly modelled on The Pride of Brexit, by Jason deCaires Taylor! Roaring like grizzled banshees, they slouch and force their way into the debating chamber, encircling the politicians who were, until a minute ago, in power. But even this is merely a distraction! Flown in by a flock of blade angels,
a battalion of Irish Famine memorial statues have been battering at the external doors, and now they break
their way through into the main chamber.

Before they can escape, several purposefully selected MPs are physically pinned down by the gaunt but heavy Irish apparitions, intent on feeding both themselves and their emaciated children: whom they grimly hold in place, to satisfy their ravenousness.
Meanwhile, delicate porous and wispy figures, resembling Claudia Fontes's Foreigners, emerge from the drains and manholes of all major cities: they meld, embrace and flow into and out of each other. They burst and flourish onto the New York Highline, in ways which echo and manifest Fontes's proposed design. Television news reporters lose all words, burst into tears, profess burning love for each other, tear off their clothes with the passionate urgency of shedding their skins, then proceed to caress, kiss and copulate. Look at 'em all: vickaterynew, in their strangeflesh.
All over the world, Riot Police are sent in to restore civic order, with truncheons and rubber bullets. To their appalled surprise, the troops find their own bodies start to melt: to morph, to blacken, to merge, like hot liquorice, so they become the writhing tentacles of a single beast.
But this Hydra finds it's up against the shock troops. Surging up from the sewers, sloughing off the shit, multiple incarnations of Rutelli's Victory emerge and stand: in each location, simultaneously, clad in seacoral armour, wielding a blade. As she severs the first neck, each coral figure is joined by another, a black-marble twin. As she severs another, they are joined by a third figure, of sheer chrysolite. Together, they lop off the other heads, and the Hydra necks

flop to the floor, in stupefied outrage, spurting pitch.
The Lynx pauses, takes a deep breath:
lines up the *piece de résistance*.
Then he utters the fateful incantation:
'You have front of house clearance'; 'stand by'; and 'go'.
A gigantic white wild horse gallops down the streets of
New York, through its towering but narrow concrete
canyons, a night mare of startling awesome beauty.
She is modelled on 'The Horse Problem' installation by
Claudia Fontes, surged into life, but even larger, and
bearing down on Times Square, to where a disengaged
stone boy scrawls sums in the dust, and stares at his screen.
Everyone is screaming, stampeding, BUT
A marble girl emerges from the crowd, walking slowly but
steadily in the opposite direction to the panicking crowds,
she covers her eyes as if she can't bear to see the fragility
of her own stance AND
The
Horse
Rears
Up
And
Back:
Into a frozen moment
A dilemma of impossible forces POISED IN SPACE
AND IT STAYS THERE
LIKE THAT

Though the girl still can't bear to look
She just draws the silence into herself
As do those who look on, amazed.
And then, after a while, she turns to the crowds,
an' says: 'Extermination
Or
Exgermination?
It is REQUIRED
You do AWAKE.'
And The Lynx nods, grunts, says:
'Willya lookatthat?
That's worth remembering.
An' there to remind you.
That when I shrug:
Atlas - an' Ayn Rand – had better look out.
You've a few things, to mull over.
Starting with: anger, and longing.
I'll bet you fancy a pint now. I do'.
The Lynx pushes his shades up his snout:
goes 'heh' to himself;
draws down his brows an' neck, an' says:
'Right. I'm off to have a cider with
The Rock Drill.
Then:
I'm back on guard.
Till the next time'. *(He disappears)*

ANNIE: *(to TANWEN)* Now's the time!
Gather your firm, an' make your move.
You've been given the chance!
So make it count! *(goes to leave)*

TANWEN: Wait! Can't you stick around?
Help me know, what to do?

ANNIE: *(archly mystical)* I have many names, pilgrim.
(Gleeful "reveal")
And one of them is Annie BYNIAETH!
(ANNIE performs a comedian's "beat".
TANWEN does not understand, is nonplussed.
ANNIE waves it away.) Paid a becso.
You'll know what to do. When the time comes.

TANWEN: *(Beat)* I don't stay alive, do I?

ANNIE: Well: nobody does, do they? Not your model.
They all run down, eventually.

TANWEN: I mean, I don't survive this. Making this "move".
Do I? Do they?

ANNIE: *(Beat)* Probably not. I don't know: I can't tell.
But no, you probably don't.
So make the most of it, eh?

(Beat) Look: I'll show up for you, one last time.
But frankly: I've got other fish to fry.
It's not all about you. It can't be.
And that's just as well.
Imagine. If it WERE! PRESSURE!!
You've got enough to deal with. Get cracking!
(She is gone)

TANWEN: *(exasperated)* Diolch yn fawr!

R2:

TANWEN, CATRIN, AISLING, DYFRIG

leading BETI ('The Firm').

They are confronted by riot police.

TANWEN starts up a rhythmic beat, like a

flamenco dancer.

The others pick it up.

TANWEN: FLOW!

(LF/X change: in slow-motion,
The Firm non-violently move,
as if in a graceful dance, through one wave
of the riot police. On to a second pressure point:
the police attempt a kettling tactic, to bunch and
confine The Firm. On a sign from BETI, they
huddle, there is one quick hug: then TANWEN
runs off. All freeze, except CATRIN, who produces
ANNIE's flask, and pours from it into a sherry
glass, which she ritualistically hands to BETI.
BETI ritualistically takes this and knocks this
back in one.
BETI is then handed a violin by DYFRIG, which
she proceeds to play appallingly and relentlessly,
advancing towards the police, who now unfreeze.
CATRIN and AISLING run off).

RIOT POLICEMAN:

Halt. You must respect our position.

Stand down. Or we will engage, forcibly.

(BETI is undeterred, adamant)

You can see our weapons,
and know that we WILL use them.

BETI: I do not. See. Your weapons.
I do not. Respect. Your position.
You're just. The rich. Man's. Army
So YOU'RE. More. Afraid. Than I am!

RIOT POLICEMAN: SNATCH SQUAD!

(Riot police attempt a Snatch Squad manoeuvre on BETI, who resists doggedly, is beaten down, gets up again, keeps playing, refuses to be moved, is clustered, forced between two shields.
She falls, and dies.
SF/X as they freeze, BONEBLACK walks out from between the cluster, to BETI. A gesture: releasing her, and he moves on through.
DYFRIG is filming all this.
The riot police unfreeze, step back, in some disarray at what they have done.)

DYFRIG: FEEL LIKE MEN NOW, DO YA?

(Then he bolts out, clutching his camera. Some chase him. ONE of the police is visibly disturbed at what he, and they, have done: pulls off his helmet, throws it away. His colleagues try to console and support him, he pushes them away. He reels off, a couple of them follow him, concerned.)

R3:

ANNIE: Lynx - The Lynx - He did it.
He fucking did it. They all did.
WE all did.
Look at 'em, Boneblack. Boneblack?
BONEBLACK! *(BONEBLACK appears)*
Breaking free:
the mayflies.
'Cos they've seen the statues do it. Set the pace.
The Lynx is right:
they can ALL shrug it off.
Obedience:
To what's killing them
(Beat)
Or they can die trying.
(Beat)

BONEBLACK: What – do you think – they'll tell?
And remember?
They live so briefly.
Will those that come after – just get puzzled?
Or disbelieve? Or be even more scared?

ANNIE: We
They
have gotta take the chance, that they won't.

Nothing ventured, nothing happens.
Just for now:
look at that lovely friction.
Trans-mission. Con-fusion.
Look at those two, drawing deep on each others' breath,
Them, tearin' open their shirts an' twiddlin'
each others' sexberries:
Look at them, amusin' their bouches
with stiffy cocky puddin';
Look at her, ecstatic at havin' her downward duct
licked an' sucked.
Boneblack:
I envy them.
We're forever separate.
We can't do that. *(She looks at him intently)*
Could we EVER do that? Could you? Did you?
Sometime in the past? Before you became –
What you are now?

BONEBLACK: I've no memory of such – things, Annie.
But then:
my business is with the memories of others.
If I had my own
I must have – lost sight of them.

ANNIE: But then what happens to you? Or me?
Do WE ever get – gathered up?
Do we just keep going?

Who do we tell OUR stories to?
Who is there to listen?

BONEBLACK: Well. I am, for you. Right now.
(He takes a step towards her)

ANNIE: Yes. And I am, for you.
(She takes a step towards him. Beat)
Is there anything you want to tell me?
Or ask? *(BONEBLACK reflects.*
Pause. He takes a step back.)

BONEBLACK: In order to comprehend something:
you have to fathom, that it is a perceptible entity:
which is - nevertheless - comprised of
opposing forces. *(Pause)*
Does that cheer you up?

ANNIE: You mean:
It's paradoxical. But possible?
Like when I say:
I AM consistent:
in SOME things?

BONEBLACK: Yes. And when you say,
that something is just as good,
as something else. But better.
It's what makes you – Lively.

ANNIE: Yes
But not alive;
Not like them.
So what are WE obedient to?
And why?

BONEBLACK: We have A Different Job.
They make memories.
But you: you have to push or pull them,
out of their comfort zone,
before they can: make memories.

ANNIE: Then: you gather them up.
When they're Breaking Black.

BONEBLACK: Yes.
But I have to have, something to gather.
That's where you come in. You're vivacious.

ANNIE: Yes.
So
we'll always be together?

BONEBLACK: Looks like it.
Just as well, we get on.

ANNIE: Yes. It's good to have you around.

BONEBLACK: It's good to have YOU around.
(He breaks the gaze, and turns away)

ANNIE: So
We have plenty of time
To try out some things

BONEBLACK: ?

ANNIE: Plenty of things *(He turns towards her)*
And some we haven't tried before
(She lets her words hang in the air. She smiles.)

R4:

(WEARHEAD watches a giant screen
of news coverage:
'BLIND WOMAN DIES IN RIOT:
POLICE STATEMENT FOLLOWS:
PROTESTS AND CLASHES INCREASING
GLOBALLY IN ALL MAJOR CITIES:
MASSIVE SOCIAL DISRUPTION:
STATE OF EMERGENCY DECLARED
WORLDWIDE'.
WEARHEAD turns it off. TANWEN enters.)

TANWEN: The doors are open – everywhere. I was able
to, just, walk in.
All your security guards have fled.
You're on your own.

WEARHEAD: *(ill, weakened, distracted)*
My kids are dead. They died.

TANWEN: I made it. I'm here. *(produces a knife)*
To call you to account.

WEARHEAD: Look, people trust me.
They know what's good for them.
They understand: that you can't make an omelette,
without breaking eggs.
They just need someone,
not scared to have the strength. To do that.

TANWEN: But what if: most of them never wanted
a fucking omelette in the first place?
And now, we can't get back,
the eggs you've broken?
Who gave YOU the right to do that?

WEARHEAD: I'm acting, in accordance with the will of the people.

TANWEN: Not my will. Not my people. Your will.
Your people. HIS will. *(Beat)*

WEARHEAD: Whose will?

TANWEN: The will you put, in the place of this -
World?
It's like Lowri
She didn't leave me willingly
She was taken away from me
What a – desecration
What a waste
Of all that.
How dare you. How dare you.
How can what we had, be wrong?
What would you put in its place?
I didn't save her. So I'm going to use the time
I have left. To save the world. From you.
You refuse to stop. You refuse to be sorry.

So I have to bring you: sorrow. Down!

(gestures: WEARHEAD obeys.
TANWEN stands behind WEARHEAD)

I think I'm gonna start: with your tongue.
(As TANWEN puts the blade to WEARHEAD's tongue, ANNIE appears in front of her.)

ANNIE: Juss sayin' - pilgrim -
all things considered
is this the smartest move you've ever made?

TANWEN: I don't NEED you, ANY MORE!
(WEARHEAD is bewildered by this,
as well as terrorized.)

ANNIE: No, you don't –
(Enter, behind ANNIE, the CONTRITE POLICEMAN,
helmetless, flanked by two of his colleagues.
TANWEN braces for a stand-off.
But there is something surprising about their focus.)

You've got them.

CONTRITE POLICEMAN: We've decided.
She's *(indicates WEARHEAD)* a liability.

ANNIE: I told you. It ain't all about you. Fortunately.
(She moves around the CONTRITE POLICEMAN)
Didn't you think: I'd also be talkin' to others? All
the time? But it's your move. *(Then: ANNIE is gone.)*

CONTRITE POLICEMAN: You can leave this. To us.

(TANWEN thinks; puts up her knife; walks between them and out.
The three POLICEMEN take steps towards WEARHEAD. From the opposite direction, so does BONEBLACK.)

R5:

M: Oh no. Oh no. We can’t have this.
I’m going to have to put things - back on track.
(to audience:) Pleased to meet you.
You want deliverance from your suffering.
I can give you that.
You want to be made new and clean.
I can do that.
Look around you:
Everything is going off the rails.
I can stop all the waste,
of space and time.
I have sympathy.
So I’m going to set you free
From the trickling indignity
Of this leaky mess called flesh.
I can save the world
From the canker
Of filth and noise and heat
That is your species.
Why put it off?
Let’s be quick and efficient about this.
We want the world to be clean and peaceful, don’t we?
So let’s do what’s necessary
And get it over with
So that something else can start

And function properly.
Let's face it:
Generally speaking, isn't 'The World As You Know It'
Overwhelmingly
Hateful?
So I'm offering you an alternative
The honourable cause, to stop the rot
Of you.
After all, who wants to be rot? Who wants to rot?
Better to burn: a quick bright flame.
Then peace. Silence. All the struggle, over.
Someone else's problem.
The process has already started
That's the nature of my - job
We just need to work together, a little while,
to see it through
You're exactly who I need, for that
At long last:
I'm very pleased to meet you.
(Enter ANNIE)

ANNIE: Hold your horses, Hecate.
Maybe they're dreaming you
But maybe, they're also dreaming me.
And I'm not overwhelmed by anything.
Except myself, occasionally.
And I bet they can guess your real names.

M: Oh, piss off, Puck. We're at a serious stage, here.

ANNIE: Now, when you SAY that, what do you MEAN by that?
Of course 'The World As They Know It' is a mess
So they gotta be reminded,
how to make it, an' keep it, a healthy mess;
To stop making 'losers', an' fencing them off;
So then they can ALL start winning.

M: They don't want to be part of a mass.
They want to be individual: different.

A: And they are. They are different.
But they're not separate.
Not like us, Manylion.
Till now, we've been separate, from them,
an' their timeframe,
an' from each other.
They ain't separate: that makes them lucky.
Helps them be prepared: for opportunities.

M: To do what? Their life has NO MEANING.
See how they behave.
They kill each other, and themselves, to make
everything more – CHEAP.
I'm helping to relieve them, of a burden.

ANNIE: It's not that their life has no meaning.
It's that they – and YOU – are giving it none.
They make 'meaning' when they try – to make
everything around them, more than the sum of its parts.
So come down off YOUR pedestal.
Stop tossin' shapes, an' pretendin' you're The Devil.
You're just strappin' on yer Doomsday Cock.
'Cos you an' me know:
The Devil don't exist.
Oh, you can speak in a minor key,
an' swish yer cape all yer want.
But a better name for you:
would be – CONTROL…

M: And you are CRAZY

ANNIE: Yes I am. And I'm right. About this.
I wanna ask the Mayflies:
why should a 'world as they know it' always be
preferable: to a world they DON'T know?
Now, that sounds like Depression speakin'!
I've seen you, out drinkin' with Depression,
hangin' around him, so you can steal his lines!
But 'What they DON'T know' is THE FUTURE.
Bein' scared of that is POINTLESS,
unless all they want outta life is a little lie down.
Which they're gonna get eventually, anyway.

Might as well have a little faith: enjoy the wakin' hours,
while they've got 'em, an' make themselves
an' others welcome.

M: But the DAMAGE.
Of their FILTH. Spreading ROT.
Don't try to tell me, there aren't some of them
that it's not worth talking to -

ANNIE: I think you're like them,
you're just scared of bein' surprised.
All the more reason, to allow yourself t'BE surprised.
Here – *(ANNIE takes M's wrist, draws him into her)*
You're welcome *(then envelops M in a long, slow, passionate kiss. M surrenders to it, then resists it).*

M: NO – (*breaks away and hits ANNIE*).

ANNIE: *(reels out, gasps, laughs: turns back:)*
C'mon then: what's your next trick?

M: *(in disarray, shocked, lifts his hands in helplessness.)*

ANNIE: You don't have to look away.
(extends her hands to him) Or turn back.
Or make the same mistake.

M: *(Quivering with contrary tensions, he recoils;*
then moves slowly, drawn towards her:
finds an embrace, finds her mouth for a kiss,
her body for a caress.)

ANNIE: See?

When you get down to it and let go –

It's nothing to be scared of.

I reckon, there's only one thing,

that's really worth investing in.

(They become aware of audience, watching them.

Pause.) Shall we - get a room?

R6:

(DYFRIG returns to the same place he sat in his first scene. He seems older. BONEBLACK watches him.

DYFRIG looks out to sea. After a while, he seems surprisingly aware of BONEBLACK, and addresses him:)

DYFRIG: I didn't make the same mistake, twice.

(BONEBLACK considers this.

Then gives DYFRIG a thumbs-up sign.

DYFRIG returns the sign to BONEBLACK).

DYFRIG: But now I'm ready. When you are.

(BONEBLACK pauses, gestures:

'Hold on there':

'The air! The clouds! sea!'

'I'll see you, later.'

'Bye for now'.

BONEBLACK leaves him.

DYFRIG looks out to sea.)

R7:

(CATRIN and AISLING: intoxicated, euphoric)

CATRIN: So let's draft - some ideas! For starters. Principles.
For a CASCADE of – of processes.
To transmit the memories. And to act on them.

AISLING: We - leave as many of the statues, as possible,
where they are.

CATRIN: Definitely! Definitely - the figures, on all the buildings.
Looking down. Watching. The lions. And definitely –
The Horse and The Girl, in Times Square.
So they redirect the traffic. Around it.
Already, there's crowds.
Making long journeys. To see it.

AISLING: We set up - a programme.
Of working, artistically AND scientifically - with air,
water,
earth
and fire.

CATRIN: And glove puppets.

AISLING: Yes! Always, particularly: the glove puppets.

CATRIN: Apparently, peoples' serotonin and dopamine levels have been boosted, all at once, to a record collective HIGH. So we need to encourage them. To direct that.

AISLING: Yes! To make choices. With radical consequences. Based on this new awareness of, of, what's around them. And what can happen. To join with –

CATRIN: Exactly. Join WITH. Not unite against.

AISLING: Exactly! We reassess the changes, that the
technology forces onto the society,
and onto the individuals, for which IT was invented.
And we reverse the flow.
We refuse, to be overwhelmed.

CATRIN: WE decide. Which patterns of behaviour
WE accelerate, and which we decelerate.
In order to live differently.

AISLING: Yes. We don't look back, with remorse.
At what we used to be.

CATRIN: But. Isn't that – quite a human thing, to do?

AISLING: We work out: what being human, MIGHT BE.
We try things out. We lose what we were!

CATRIN: That's why we tend, to fear changes.
Even when we want them.

AISLING: We've been gifted ANOTHER CHANCE!
We owe it, to ourselves: to dream ourselves,
into - new shapes.
Better versions.

CATRIN: But we're not - programmed to do that.
We're not caterpillars. Or tadpoles. We don't moult.

AISLING: But! We can put our minds, to drive towards it.
We can SOAR!

CATRIN: And we can't foresee, or determine,
what these changes will be. *(Beat)*
In some ways, we lose control.

AISLING: We lose control. We rebuild ourselves.

CATRIN: Hey. Where's Tanwen?

AISLING:

CATRIN: Do you think - she will be able to - ?

R8:

(Sounds of crowds, sirens)

TANWEN: *(lurking, crouching, emerging from shadows. She has a developed a feral wiliness)*
So:
I could be –
on a countdown.
But then – aren't we all?
You just hope you've made the best story you can,
for when the time comes.
(Sounds of protest, rioting, suppression)
They say,
you should never give a sword,
to a man who can't dance:
I bet they don't have that rule
when they hand out the truncheons
and the riot shields
and the rubber bullets.
(She sees something. Deep intake of breath)
Hey officer!
You and your BOYS wanna try doing that: to me?
Let's see how you deal
with someone else, who's not afraid
Let's make some memories
But I oughta warn you:
I've got the edge:

I've got hope
And you don't seem to;
Else you wouldn't be here
Doing this
To them.
You see, I know someone
Who's standing by;
He's ready for one of us:
And I have my story, ready for him:

Learn from the past,
Seize the present,
Clear a path for the future.

I would PREFER that you take off your helmet
Rather than I
have to break
what's underneath it
But the choice is yours:
Bravery,
Or Slavery:
Slavery to someone else's story;
Or bravery to make and tell your own.
So c'mon fucker
Either: you can tell me, YOUR story
or
Let's dance:
It's Show Time.

(TANWEN assumes combat position.
She freezes and is illuminated differently and/or silhouetted, so she appears as if a statue.
Then the lights fast fade.)

((((((((()))))))))))

(Possible curtain call and play-out music:
'Statue in the Square' (2025) by Kae Tempest)

Director-Dramatist's Foreword to *Land of My Fathers* by *David Ian Rabey*

What happens in *Land of My Fathers?*

MI6 agent Owain has just deactivated a terrorist cell in Huddersfield when he receives a summons to a new mission. His Chief of Operations briefs him on how he will join an MI6 team of fellow Welshmen: Iestyn, a former British Army soldier stationed in Belfast, and Cai, the nephew of Iestyn's former comrade. They will carry out investigative actions in Afghanistan and Iraq, pretending to be security contractors: this professional status will put them beyond the remit of international law, but also beyond official assistance in an emergency. The Chief also warns Owain of doubts about the fundamental loyalties of Cai, who comes from a family tradition of disobedience. The trio have an informal meeting, then they fly out to Afghanistan, to investigate reports that a rogue British Army unit has established a protection racket amongst local Afghan drug-runners. They locate and terminate this unit. Their second mission takes them to Iraq. They reflect on the grim ironies of their work, in relation to what they observe, but try to keep their spirits high. Iestyn expresses to Owain his growing distrust of Cai. Cai reports they are to seek out a guerilla bomb unit which is hiding in the hills beyond Baghdad. Iestyn suspects Cai may be luring Owain and Iestyn into a trap.

The trio head into the hills, locate the bombers' hideout, and kill them. Contrary to concern that the gunshots may attract more enemy presences, Cai insists the trio head further up into the hills. He leads them to a cave, the entrance to which is guarded by his mutilated uncle, and which leads to a network of abandoned tunnels. Cai reveals to Owain and Iestyn that, over the last four years, he has been making secret visits to his uncle here. They have worked together in the tunnels to develop a gallery of uncanny effigies associated with an idiosyncratic form of death worship. Recoiling from these, Iestyn blurts out the doubts surrounding Cai's loyalties, and the instruction to kill him if his disloyalty were confirmed. Cai is appalled by their willingness to do this, which he takes as a personal betrayal. Iestyn claims his loyalty was simply to following orders. Cai lures Iestyn into an apparently comradely embrace; then kills him in a homicidal rage. Owain voices his own contrasting loyalty and emergent homoerotic attraction to the distraught Cai and risks a contrasting embrace. Owain and Cai reject their military status and duties and abscond together.

Objectives and contexts:

Yes, it's a provocative choice of title and theme. I'm not Welsh-born, though, for the record, my maternal grandparents worked, met and married in Aberystwyth. From 1985, I did similarly.

This play began with two things.

Firstly: the challenge from Richard Harrington to write a play for three men: ideally, to form a basis for Harrington, Russell Gomer and Richard Lynch to rekindle their onstage partnership and rapport as had been previously forged in several stage plays for Ed Thomas. Female characters are integral to my other original dramatic work. So, this was a further challenge. A triangle of forces, a trio of characters (whatever their gender or sexuality), is likely to shift in its dynamics in response to events: relocation, alliance, suspicion, betrayal, attraction, protectiveness, antagonism, cohesion, separation: and, possibly, sacrificial elimination. Love. And Hate.

Secondly: the insight that the dominant political metaphor for our time is outsourcing: the forcing of a distance in time and space between action and consequences. Outsourcing can make an otherwise unacceptable and illegal process of dispossession into a source of centralized profit. Its reverse-telescope perspective normalizes and conceals long-term catastrophic human disposability, in order to establish and maintain a systematic short-term profitability. This benefits only a few plutocrats, who promise a purported "security" which actually demands a systematic destabilization of the wider whole ('We came, we saw, we fracked'). As Naomi Klein observes, this process of enclosure begins in the Middle Ages, when common lands in England were transformed into privately held commodities, and the role of land changed:

> its role was no longer to benefit the community – with shared access to communal grazing, food, and firewood – but to increase crop yields and therefore profits for individual landowners. Once physically and legally enclosed, the soil began to be treated as a machine, whose role was to be as productive as possible. (Klein 2023: 40-1)

The identification and preservation of so-called 'vital national interests' has led to the extension of what Naomi Klein terms The Shock Doctrine, the deliberate and traumatic destabilization of nation states with seizable resources, and what Stephen Armstrong terms 'War plc', the corporate privatization of war through the employment of security contractors by multinational companies. These security contractors are more cost effective than soldiers, engaged to carry out specified tasks, after which their contracts and costs end. Crucially, they are also not subject to international military law.

Any market-driven exercise in restructuring – whether the political and commercial resources of a foreign country, or that of a domestic society or institution – identifies money as the determining factor to ensure a form of stability, which in fact makes increasingly and systematically precarious the existence of anyone or anything not quantifiably contributing maximally to an increasingly centralized profit. Unfortunately, since the play's premiere, there are even more instances of what it identifies: so-called "developers" seeing dollar signs in the rubble of clearances which displace indigenous people.

So, what if a team of MI6 spies were ordered to go undercover and pass themselves off as security contractors, as the most effective means to further the latest not-entirely-transparent configuration of 'national interests'? Men who were resolute, resourceful, independent, but strategically unpredictable, and so a potential liability. And what if they were Welsh? Such men might, and might not, be thought and made useful in "national interests".

> In December 2006, Plaid Cymru used the Freedom of Information Act to obtain figures on school visits by the Army Recruitment Division for 2005-6. The figures showed that schools in the most deprived areas of Wales were visited 50 per cent more often than those in affluent areas. Schoolchildren in Swansea received an average of ten visits a year, while those in the wealthy Vale of Glamorgan received not at all. Plaid Cymru asked the Welsh Assembly to ban the army from schools, but their request was denied. (Armstrong 2008: 212)

In Gary Raymond's 'personal journey through the history of Welsh literature', *Abandon All Hope*, he is arraigned by the ghost of Raymond Williams, who tells him 'Wales is too complex to stand under one banner, and yet we feel we need that banner to be noticed. Simple messages'. Gary immediately replies: 'That's politics, not culture' (Raymond 2024: 42). But his overall suggestion is that it is both.

In *Land of My Fathers*, the objective was to write a 'rewilded' state-of-the-nation play (to apply a term I have coined for Jez Butterworth's *Jerusalem*: in Rabey 2015: 138), in which the characters' adventures make them start to ask: what are we loyal to, and why? What's our place in the world? What's at the bottom of the power, and violence, that people want?

Backstory:

Richard Lynch had attained international acclaim in the title role of Karl Francis's film *Milwr Bychan* (1986), which I had seen in its premiere screening at the Edinburgh Festival that year. In this film, Lynch plays Wil Thomas, a Valleys tearaway who is lured into signing up with the British Army and is posted to Belfast. Russell Gomer plays his companion, Corporal Wright. Thomas's experiences as an ostensible "peacekeeper" on the streets of another nation drive him into trauma, incarceration and a principled stand of disobedience against the brutalizing imperialistic totalitarianism of the British Army's torturous principles. The physical brutality and electro-convulsive shock treatment to which he is subjected is intended to break his will, but in fact they strengthen his resolve, and make manifest some of the formerly implicit oppression.

My first thought towards a narrative was a speculation about the subsequent lives of Wil Thomas and the former Corporal Wright, in the present day, as they were joined by a third, younger MI6 operative, charged to investigate alleged shifts in loyalties. This yielded a first version: a text workshopped at Gregynog Hall in Newtown, with Lynch, Gomer and Aneirin Hughes. Notwithstanding their remarkable performances, the event exposed to me some slackness in the texture and gear shifts of my writing. I returned to the story, when an opportunity for staging was presented, at a time when Harrington and Lynch were professionally unavailable, and I brought to bear new rigour and ideas.

Russ Gomer could present a latter-day Corporal Wright, alongside two younger colleagues, one of whom could be Cai Thomas, the nephew of Milwr Bychan's Will Thomas (however, a reimagined version of the character might reappear, in a startling, scarcely recognizable and literally unseen form). The musculature of the play might be leaner, its political reference points necessarily updated, its texture rendered differently, in more burgeoningly surreal and mythic terms.

Formal influences and guiding principles:

I have acknowledged earlier in this volume the importance of my attendance in November 2017 of Damien Hirst's exhibition at Venice Biennale, *Treasures from the Wreck of the Unbelievable*. Hirst's fantastic creations seemed to chime with some of my own imagined artifacts, and beckon them outwards, and into even stranger forms (however: I had imagined and written *The Spirit of Defeat*, and *Land of My Fathers* had been staged, before I first encountered, startlingly, Hirst's statue *Anatomy of an Angel* at Houghton Hall in Norfolk in 2018). I regularly commenced each bout of drafting and honing the script by playing the cd by P. J. Harvey, *Let England Shake* (2011), to provide rapid and appropriate emotional relocation. Some of that recording's musical and lyrical atmosphere has doubtlessly infused the play.

I also realized that my story's excavatory story-arc resonated with that of another acknowledged influence, David Rudkin's *The Sons of Light*, a play I co-directed with John O'Brien in 1990. In my later work on Rudkin, I discovered (thanks to James Reynolds) and deployed the term *katabasis*. Rudkin's work provides several examples of the dramatic process, in which figure and landscape grow into each other, and go down into darkness together: a process which, although daunting, proves to be not necessarily an occasion for contraction and recoil. It may instead be a process of *katabasis* – a conscious risk and willed plunge downwards and inwards - which offers some reconstitution, which is existentially necessary.

Development:

I realize in retrospect that all of my plays insist that identity is not fixed; they depict attempts to break some fatalistic, deterministic cycle of inherited values and self-partitioning, whilst also testifying to the painful difficulty of doing so ('If I blame my mother and I blame my dad / They'll just blame their mother and blame their dad': *The Hanging Judge*). My son Ryan's casual reference over supper one night, to 'the minotaur of anticipation squatting in the maze of logic', may still stand as his best wisecrack to date; it is run a close second by his reference to 'skating on the ice of hopelessness, like a hot penguin': two images and phrases too good to be forgotten, or unshared. In fact, the story of Theseus and the Minotaur, the motif of the labyrinth and surprising forms discovered in the depths and walls of a cave have always haunted me; but I had no foreknowledge that the journey of *Land of My Fathers* would lead into the mouth and depths of a cave until I wrote that section automatically. Up to that point, I had researched landscapes (Afghanistan and Iraq) which I had not personally visited, and forms of combat I hope I never witness.

My three characters are literally and metaphorically scrambling through a bombsite of cultural fragments. They desperately, pathetically, endearingly, foolishly try to construct national affiliations and masculine identities through some frantic bricolage of the fragments they find: James Bond films, music, comics, popular culture, foundation myths, nihilistic detachment, hedonism, narcotics. Stage manager Maisie Baynham pointed out that Gomer's character, Iestyn Wright, repeatedly presents, in full confidence, images of what it means to be a man, which the other two cannot make match with their different generation's experiences. But all three of the characters are, in different ways, dangerously, even lethally, reactionary; and, in different ways, they prove surprisingly and courageously inventive. These moments may assist the audience to a discovery of surprising forms of respect, for figures they might otherwise understandably consider abject. They also try to suggest that the identities and systems created by humans can, and must, be changed.

I confess I had been suspicious of digital forms of scenography when my experiences of examples had predominantly been of literal and flatly representational images, slammed and pasted up, devoid of depth. I rapidly rethought my prejudices when I saw Piotr Woycicki's revelatory work for Karoline Gritzner's workshop tango-based performance project, *Thoughts Which Can Be Danced* (2014). Peter's work demonstrated a rare inventiveness, not least in how he discovered responsive and surreal images which could morph unpredictably into one another. I sensed how this could assist, and crucially inform, a production of *Land of My Fathers*, which insists on rapid transitions in international location and tone, veering from a pragmatic brutalism to a hallucinogenic rapture, from grinding squalor to consciously ludicrous idealism, all to be located and expressed as viscerally as possible. I will always be grateful to Piotr for his acceptance of my invitation to contribute, and his tirelessly inventive work.

Naomi Klein follows Hannah Arendt in considering how 'it is when everyday people lose their capacity for internal dialogue and deliberation, and find themselves only able to regurgitate slogans and contradictory platitudes, that great evil occurs'. It is when people lose the ability to imagine the perspectives and physical presences of absent others – an individual(ized) thoughtlessness – that totalitarianism and evil take hold: 'Put differently, we should not fear hearing voices in our heads – we should fear their absence' (Klein 2023: 66). I suggest that Theatre is a collective means to reconsider, challenge and imagine: and to provoke and encourage what Klein identifies as 'deliberation, debate and elasticity' (*ibid.*) where the stakes are civilizational. As she subsequently observes: no one makes themselves: 'we all make and unmake one another' (*ibid.*, 326.)

> The known world is crumbling. That's okay. It was an edifice stitched together with denial and disavowal, with unseeing and unknowing, with mirrors and shadows. It needed to crash. Now, in the rubble, we can make something more reliable, more worthy of our trust, more able to survive the coming shocks. (*ibid.*, 342)

Now is an important time for us all to re-examine our national and international loyalties: to think about who we are allying ourselves with: how, on whose terms, and in whose ultimate interests? And with a sense of myth: what is it that might turn out, to be lying under the familiar surfaces of our re-presented daily lives and landscapes, waiting to be acknowledged, and make its claims?

One way is for people to get together, outside their own houses, screens and phones: take some time to gather round a story: let it unfold, share some laughs, share some fears, laugh at their fears, ask some questions: about the values we're expected to live by, and how we might change them. That's being social.

REFERENCES:

Armstrong, Stephen (2008) *War PLC*. London: Faber.

Klein, Naomi (2023) *Doppelganger: A Trip into The Mirror World*. London: Penguin.

Rabey, David Ian (2015) *The Theatre and Films of Jez Butterworth.* London: Bloomsbury.

Reynolds, James (2015) 'Going Underground' in Reynolds, James, and Smith, Andy W. (eds.), *Howard Barker's Theatre*. London: Bloomsbury pp. 149-168.

LAND OF MY FATHERS

by

David Ian Rabey

Land of My Fathers was first rehearsed in February 2018 in the basement of Little Man Coffee Shop, Cardiff, with Jack Hammett in the role of Owain. This was a Lurking Truth / Gwir sy'n Llechu production scheduled by Aberystwyth Arts Centre, for performances in early March. However, the performances were postponed because of the Arts Centre's closure on account of extreme weather ('The Beast from The East'), and rescheduled for 10-12 May 2018 as an Arts Centre presentation at Theatr y Castell, Aberystwyth (with kind permission of Aberystwyth University Department of Theatre, Film and Television Studies) with the following company:

Cast:

OWAIN	OLIVER MORGAN-THOMAS
CAI	HUW BLAINEY
IESTYN / THE CHIEF	RUSSELL GOMER

Director:	DAVID IAN RABEY
Producer:	CERIANN WILLIAMS
Digital Scenography and Animations:	PIOTR WOYCICKI
Stage Manager:	MAISIE BAYNHAM
Associate Director:	IZZY RABEY

Assistant Stage Managers: ELLA PURVIS-HISLOP;
DAWN TOLAND, SEREN TUSON

Programme Design: EMILY DYBLE-KITCHIN

Poster Design: CHRIS STEWART from a photo by KEITH MORRIS

With thanks to: Becky Mitchell; Gill Ogden; Richard Harrington, Russell Gomer and Richard Lynch for inspiration; Russell, Richard and Aneirin Jones for workshopping the first draft in a performance at Gregynog Hall, Newtown; and Kai Bools, Tim Martin-Jones and Mart-Matteus Kampus for assistance in workshopping the digital scenography of the production at a later stage.

A British psychiatrist wrote on electroshock therapy back in 1940, 'The introverted schizophrenic or melancholic may be likened to a walled city which has closed its gates and refuses to trade with the rest of the world'. Then, a 'breach is blown in the wall, and relations with the world are re-established. Unfortunately, we cannot control the amount of damage done in the bombardment'.

Naomi Klein, *The Shock Doctrine*.

Only the love of comrades sweetens all,
Whose laughing spirit will not be outdone.

Ivor Gurney, 'Sonnets 1917' ('Servitude'),
Severn and Somme

If I can't be a peaceful man,
I'll just be who I am;
If I can't get just what I want,
I'll just get what I can.

John Martyn, '*Make No Mistake*'

I grow taller
On my father's back
Yet still he rides me
To a certain end

What sin has been committed
That the land will not forget
What creeping revenge
Screaming in the rock
Driving us to crash
In a re-enactment
An atonement

And I will teach you
How to dance
To dance freestyle;
For your partner, Death,
Knows only the tango;
A freestyle flicker
Through a dark stone hall.

John O'Brien, '*Taking Steps*'

Part One

Opening exordium: The Company (Oliver Morgan-Thomas foreground): Russell Gomer as Iestyn (in cheerless hotel room). Photos by Keith Morris.

Music: something which exhilaratingly approximates a James Bond film or similar action movie. A valuable reference point here might be provided by the full-throttle John Barry homage that is 'All the Time in the World' by Southside Johnny and La Bamba's Big Band, from the CD Grapefruit Moon.

We Open In Huddersfield: on an MI6 and SAS covert action. Three figures, clad entirely in black (boots, jumpers, combats, ski masks) edge around the playing space; follow-spots move over them and the audience. The three figures do not interact with each other, but their stealth gradually uncoils into the decisive and succinct actions of trained combat with invisible assailants, en route *to fulfilling some larger purpose. They then have to escape their immediate settings, possibly meeting and repelling further opposition; they complete their missions and each finally permit themselves a differently idiosyncratic, stylish flourish as closure to a job well done, as the track fades, or ends. Two of the figures disappear as their lights go out. The third finds the single remaining spotlight, enjoys it, pulls off his mask.*

(Words in brackets are unspoken: intended to assist the reader to a sense of intention.)

OWAIN: Quick in, an' back out.
Back out FASTER. Stealth be damned. Shortest line.
Last ditch: bastard with gun and whistle.
Kick the whistle into the roof of his mouth. He hangs on, shooting wild.
Go for the mouth again, find the brittle hinge. Fuck!
He blocks me so I hook my thumb in his eye socket, the squishy angle, my other hand grabs his billiards, pulls and twists: he howls an' drops the gun.
BUT: he blindsides me with a lucky kick as he goes down. He's about to stamp on my hands, snap the fingers, so I curl up. I am the Feral Razorblade Hedgehog an' I prove it. I roll away, my hand finds: a brick. Harder than the flesh which he has to defend or attack. So I give him the brick.
I BESTOW it upon him.
I give him:
The Full Benefit Of The Brick.
My left ear still rings from the kick, but I shake away pain, surprise an' anger. I vanish. I find the limits
of the light, squeeze into the dark.
I am the Twisted Slink, furnace
forged to show the stupidity of sight.
Put a pistol in the hand of any man.
He will begin to toss the shapes of James, son of Bond.
The hand will lead, the spine will stretch, the feet will spread; the buttocks will tighten, the head will tilt, the brows will darken with slyness an' power.

I include myself in this. I feel the halo of the crosswires,
the Benediction of the Seeping Red.
We drink it in with our father's spunk.
I clean up the job in Huddersfield. An active cell.
Meeting in an old mill building.
We hose down and lock up. Then I get the word: back
for a briefing. Somethin' is blowin' down.

(Spot up on CAI, apart)

CAI: 'Dare to be a Daniel
Dare to stand alone
Dare to have a purpose firm
And dare to make it known.'

(THE CHIEF, seated, holds a file: he flicks through it.)

CHIEF: File on Cai Thomas. Impeccable training record.
Never knew his father.
But. There's an uncle.
Did a tour of duty in Belfast in the 80s.
Welsh Light Infantry. Put on trial for murder.
Ten weeks' solitary confinement.
Given electro-convulsive shock therapy. He was nineteen.

OWAIN: Who'd he kill?

CHIEF: Shot an Irish kid, who had a knife.
The uncle lost the nerve when his mate went down.
Dodging missiles. So he shot the pack leader.

OWAIN: Didn't wing him?

CHIEF: Then it gets messy.
The uncle's arrested, an' stops speaking English.
Says, he's 'not a Brit', he's 'Welsh'.
And he keeps speakin' Welsh. Ten weeks
solitary make most men crack.
But he was in for half as long again.

CAI: 'Not guilty, Sir. I didn't do anything I wasn't paid to do.
If I'm guilty, Sir, so are you'.

CHIEF: The uncle took the pressure like a trained field
operative. Not only did he take it; he gave it back.

CAI: *(to the audience)* The CIA counterintelligence manual
states, Quote: 'those who have withstood pain are
more difficult to handle by other methods.
The effect has been not to repress the subject
but to restore his confidence and maturity'. Unquote.

OWAIN: So he's drummed out. End of story?

CHIEF: Oh no. After two years in prison,
he drifts back to the valleys, hits the bottle.
(He) Lives at his auntie's for a spell, gets a couple
o' nights in jail for Saturday night scraps. Then he
cleans up his act. Finds a job as a gravedigger.

CAI: World without eyelids
World without lips
Amen.

CHIEF: Thomas's uncle goes the way of many an
ex-squaddie. He joins a commercial security company.
Those who offer 'crisis management',
'public service, in a private sphere'.

OWAIN: Outsourcing.

CHIEF: The way forward.
The US government learnt its lesson in
New Orleans, after Katrina.
The boots on the ground weren't soldiers, nor
police. Armed security teams. Licensed to use lethal
force: 'where necessary'.
(Rises from his chair)
Your 'Private Contractors' are more COST
EFFECTIVE than your soldiers.
When a job ends, so do the costs.
No liabilities if things go wrong.

Less grief all round. Then. On an assignment in Iraq. Thomas's uncle disappears.
No trace. *(as has CAI)*

OWAIN: Maybe Isis got him.

CHIEF: Maybe he got Isis. In his blood.
Three years ago, we enlist the uncle's colleague from the army, ex-Corporal Iestyn Wright, to work alongside young Cai Thomas, the nephew.
Inside commercial security operations.
But Iestyn Wright and young Cai Thomas are OUR men: in counter-intelligence.
We establish them as a team,
working in Afghanistan and Iraq.

OWAIN: Cai's tracing his uncle's footprints.
Under cover of being a 'mercenary' - ?

CHIEF: Dirty word. Your private security contractor says, he is not a mercenary.
Because he can pick his tasks and causes.
He says: that's more than your
average soldier is allowed to do.

OWAIN: Or Thomas and Wright; for that matter.

CHIEF: Yes. Or, indeed, you. Pritchard.

Thomas and Wright report to us,
on the operations of these private security firms,
from the places they go. These companies are
commercial enterprises. So they're not bound by
government or military regulations.

OWAIN: So they're undercover, infiltrating the security
contractors and feeding back to military intelligence.
But they've no call on official back-up, or fire-power?

CHIEF: If they fall into enemy hands, there are *(Beat)*
no international conventions regulating their
detainment. But. This way they CAN go places
where official forces can't.

OWAIN: Smart.

CHIEF: But Wright has gut feelings. Uneasy.
About Cai Thomas. You're to join them; work
alongside Thomas in some potential crisis situations.
Get close to Cai: get inside his head.

OWAIN: Sir?

CHIEF: He's made some private trips to Iraq,
on unspecified personal business. Wright thinks,

what if? Under the deep cover, there's a volcano?
What if the vanished uncle has been turned
by Al-Qaeda? Or his nephew?

OWAIN: Pulling Cai back into the family tradition?
Once a rebel, always a rebel?

CHIEF: Loose cannon or smart bomb?
We need you to check him out. We might soon
need him, here on home turf.

OWAIN: Why, sir? *(Attempts humour)*
Has someone struck oil in Blaenau Ffestiniog?

CHIEF: (*Mirthlessly*) 'Ho ho ho'.
[*lines in first performances:*
After Brexit, Theresa will call a whole new
'ball game'. No time for U-turns, or European
Human Rights. *These should be replaced by
agreed updated references to political
opportunism.*] We can get Thomas and Wright
involved, as consultants to armed security teams in
the new British fields of operation, if they're not
burnt out. But we need to make sure they bring
the right things home.

(Lights fade on The Chief. Sounds of a city street.)

OWAIN: (*direct, intimate*) So I set up a meeting in a Pub in Canton: The Robin Hood.
I arrange to meet Thomas and Wright together.
Thomas arrives first, strangely cheerful.
Known to his friends as 'The Beast of Bedwas'.
(Sounds of the pub.)

CAI: I love a good bar.
It's a place to step outside o' time.
Ever been to New York?

OWAIN: No.

CAI: There's a bar, where you can drink a dry martini, an' look down from the 25th floor onto Manhattan: an' you see the American Dream. *(Beat)*
It's fightin' on rooftops.

OWAIN: Yer what?

CAI: Fightin', on the fuckin' rooftops, mun.
Now, you ask some English twat from the so-called "Home Counties", when he was a kid, what did he do for 'an adventure'.
He'll say 'I'd play in the loft, when mummy and daddy had gone out'.
That's the English for excitement: 'tic' in the attic, Narnia wardrobes. Furtive. Americans are different.

No shame. They just wanna fight: together, upfront.
In the overworld.

OWAIN: The what?

CAI: Up in the overworld, fighting the underworld.
Up the stairs, from the street, to the rooves:
the motor rooms an' water tanks.
Where you can grapple an' slug it out:
round the wires an' chimneys. The DC an'
Marvel comics suddenly make complete sense.
It's fuckin' terrific.

OWAIN: You reckon? So woss the Welsh dream, then?

CAI: To be the hero of two worlds. *(Beat)*
Didn't yer read yer *Mabinogion*?

OWAIN: What you drinkin'?

CAI: You're OK, here's reinforcements.

IESTYN: Hiya, lads.

OWAIN: *(self-introduction)* (I'm) Owain Pritchard.

IESTYN: Iestyn Wright. *(handshake)*
Two pints, is it? *(He goes to the bar)*

CAI: So where've you been?

OWAIN: Last five years in Hereford *(i.e. SAS)*.

CAI: 'The Regiment'? An' where'd you START? Cadets?

OWAIN: None where I lived.

CAI: Cymdeithas yr Iaith?

OWAIN: Not me. My brother –

CAI: I fuckin' hate Cymdeithas yr Iaith.

OWAIN: Well, I wuz never convinced -

CAI: No, I really fuckin' hate their slimy balls.
College tossers, CND cunts.
Muesli guerrillas.
Couldn't fight their way out a branch of Habitat.
Stuff the short-legged hipsters drunk on Saunders Lewis. Gimme the boys as mean business.

OWAIN: Meaning -

CAI: Meaning, don't you ever wish: this soil beneath us, would rise up, an' spit out the invaders who are

poisoning our land?
If it does not: why is it worth our loyalty?
Is it 'PLAYING A LONG GAME'?
Or is it just STUPID? PASSIVE? An' INERT?
How foolish have WE become? EXACTLY?

OWAIN: Erm –

IESTYN: *(returning)* Oh, Cai's doin' 'is Cayo act.

CAI: That's what we used to say in Meibion Glyndwr.
And sometimes I'd use the same arguments
in the SWP. I infiltrated 'em both.

OWAIN: You were in the SWP?

CAI: *(with contempt)* The "Trotskies".
An' then, the speaker would say somethin' like:
'Do you think I have all the answers?
I do not; an' maybe, you do not. This is
because: we are Living The Contradictions.
We are sleepers, in the belly of the whale.
But: we await the moment. To start the fire'.

OWAIN: Like Pinocchio.

CAI: Wot?

IESTYN: Pinocchio?

OWAIN: He started a fire.
In the belly of the whale.
Probably: by rubbin' 'is nose against somethin'.
He musta found somethin' DOWN there,
as wasn't wet. *(Beat)*
As wasn't 'is nose.

CAI: 'As wasn't 'is nose'? *(Thinks: 'idiot')*

OWAIN: That's it, mun.
Just as well 'e WEREN'T a real live boy just yet, eh?
If 'e 'ad a been real, his nose woulda
BLED with all that rubbin', 'fore he could start the fire. Thass one of yer problems with people,
I mean people-people, too fuckin' inflammable.

CAI: Yeh well, we found ways round that with the air strikes on Mosul. *(Beat)*
Where'd they train you? Pentre Sali Mali?

OWAIN: *(snaps back with his own unexpected performance)*
I will ignore that slur on the vigilance of my colleagues in the Dyfed-Powys police, an' their Terrorism and Domestic Extremism Division: several of whom I know personally. I am proud to raise a glass with them. I toast their painstaking

surveillance of half-fried eco-bandits: them as rattle the ringpulls in their body piercings to ward off the third runway, in the badlands between Tal-y-Bont and the Dyfi Valley. Or, as it's known locally, The Gaza Strip.

IESTYN: To the blue-clad mountain men of Dyfed-Powys. *(Drinks)*

CAI: And in memory of the Association of Chief Police Officers.
Who had the right idea, till The Parker Report put them on hold. But they'll be back.

OWAIN: What idea?

CAI: Monitoring and tackling domestic extremism. The ACPO provided this brilliant strategic interface for the National Extremism Tactical Coordination Unit; the Welsh Extremism and Counter-Terrorism Unit; and the National Public Order Intelligence Unit. See the BEAUTY of it? The Association of Police Officers wasn't a Public body, it was a private limited company.
So those three units were exempt from 'freedom of information' laws, an' all the guff about 'public accountability'.
Even though they were funded by the Home Office

and deployed police officers from regional forces. Best of all, they built up a DNA database of over a million people not yet proved guilty, an' put two fingers up to the European Convention of Human Rights. *(Beat.)* I don't mock those boys. With that tactical agility an' foresight, they are the FUTURE. *(Beat)* Whether some of them know it or not.

OWAIN: So: d'you reckon that's the future?
Complete DNA databanks?

CAI: 'Course I do. Till we get the chance to implant the microchips. People will queue up for it, now security is more important than privacy. Anyone who doesn't, must have something - unpatriotic - to hide. First step in our job: know the future. Second step: *(punches his hand)* hit anything stopping it.

IESTYN: (*Proposing a toast*)
To maintaining security: home and away.
Cymru am byth.

OWAIN: *(Trying his hand)* Yeah.
Mind you, my brother an' some of his old
Cymdeithas mates, an' the Meibion monkeys,
they useta give me a hard time,
sayin' me an' the Hereford boys were basically
protectin' British interests: which strangely enough

always turn out to be the interests of South East Metropolitan England. *(Beat)*
That's what they useta say.

CAI: No, no. You see: you and me and Iestyn,
we're working to CONFINE the problems
to the major English cities. Look round you.
No one's trying to paralyze the country by
sticking a dirty bomb in Cwmgiedd, are they?
So far, no riots or suicide bombers in Brithdir.

OWAIN: Yeah, but. When the dirty bomb hits Brum.
Any scorched-barmy mutant survivors will come
across on the A458.
For plunder an' pillage. Spreadin' plague.

CAI: Which is why we have to stop the dirty bombs.
Or at worst (*beat*) CONTAIN them.

OWAIN: So, what's your plans, for after all this, then?
You savin' up for a little cottage in Aberdaron?

CAI: Too near the Irish Sea for my liking.

IESTYN: No one keeps a welcome for the likes of us.

CAI: I'm not lookin' fer one.

OWAIN: So what do you want?

CAI: *(Beat. He sizes him up.)* The same as you do.
Answer your own question.

OWAIN: *(An intent address, to audience)*
Smart. Gets me tryin' to formulate what *I* want.
Thomas gives me his famous shit-eatin' grin.
That pause is designed to leave me danglin'.
Like a mouse with no legs.
So I grow a pair.
An' I think: OK:
I want to get out of the valleys towns.
I want: something beyond the Saturday nights
when the streets become the bowl:
in which the whole town threw up.
Thass where I lived.
You are now entering: the Borough of Cwm Puke.
No plughole, just puke.
Where all the country puked, an' contained its puke.
Walkin' through puke till you become:
Walkin' Puke.
(Beat)
Cities: are where you get away from that.
You 'ave to step over the occasional dosser,
an' once in a while, dodge or
thump some sad screamer.
But thass better than turning INTO a dosser or a

sad screamer; which is what happens to you
if you stay in Cwm Puke.
If you have the money, the City is good things:
surprisin' times. Sharing those good things
with NEW people who ain't had to watch you grow up.
Discoverin' the world; its taste: full, an' ripe an'
never fully fathomed. Somethin' worth fighting for.
(Beat)
But it has to be defended.
'Gainst those who'd blow it up.
Blast us back to the puke bowl, an' the Middle Ages.
What do they have to put in the place of all
that - promise? The Saturday Night Goat Slaughter?
Thanks but no. I already gave.
(To CAI) Like you say. Deep down: *Cymru am byth.*

CAI: Sure. But don't ever get soft.

OWAIN: 'Course not.

IESTYN: We lost some friends along the way. Good friends.

CAI: We learned, we need our distance.
We know about bein' men.
What are the tricks of bein' a man, Owain?

OWAIN: *(Beat. Aware he's being set up for a punchline, but deciding to go along with it)*

I don't know, what are the tricks of bein' a man - ?

CAI: Shut up and earn the money.
Never hesitate in a doorway.
Be charmin' to everyone you meet.
But also have a plan to kill them.

OWAIN: And so I'm in.
Two weeks later, the three of us are off on a plane
to Afghanistan.
On the way to Kabul, they tell me what to expect.

(On the plane: they slowly and steadily move forwards together)

IESTYN: Afghanistan is a warped and horrific expedition
into the most outrageous forms of human existence.
It is like being shot out of a smelly dust cannon;
through wet plastic sheeting; and into a fast-forward
snuff video version of *Mad Max*.
And I said, after the last time,
I would definitely: DO IT AGAIN!!

OWAIN: We've "a contract" to protect three British salesmen.
They're selling equipment to the Afghan labs
that manufacture heroin –

CAI: Back in the nineties, Afghanistan's poppy fields

produce three quarters of the world's opium.
Then in 2000, the Taliban decides: the country's drugs trade goes against the teachings of Islam.
So they outlaw the poppy farming.
And destroy the heroin labs –

IESTYN: An' if anyone objects, the Taliban kills 'em; burns their land, an' destroys their stock.
End o' the twentieth century,
Afghan opium production is stamped out -

CAI: Then in 2001, the Taliban are shoved out of power, an' over the border.
Some Afghan farmers uncover the poppy they've been hidin', an' go back to milkin'
their most profitable cash cow.
By 2003 Afghanistan is back on top, as the main international producer of opium –

IESTYN: But this time their income gets topsliced
by the Taliban, who have overcome their religious scruples; an' al-Qaeda start up protection rackets on the poppy farmers, the heroin labs
an' drug traffickers -

CAI: The Afghan trade in heroin gets supported
by government Officials drawin' back-handers.
There'll always be a market: to get you off

your face, at home and abroad.

IESTYN: To make life bearable, in a country that's going to shit.
Offer people that, an' you'll never want for friends.
Or enemies, who want a slice of what you've got.

CAI: But you have to stay watchful.

IESTYN: So watchful, you end up needin' somethin'
to help you relax at night.

OWAIN: So we're playin' nursemaids to – SALESMEN –
who are equipping the Afghan heroin labs?

IESTYN: Well, no one wants the boys in the white coats
to do a shoddy job. Cuts across everyone's interests.
Kandahar has its own counter-narcotics unit:
but all the staff can be blackmailed. (*Trying to hail a taxi*)
They live in the area. An' their families are easy targets.

CAI: And. We think there's a British army unit
that 'ave "gone native".
Trying to move in on the Taliban's protection patch:
usin' their tactics.

IESTYN: That's upsetting EVERYONE.
Threatens the delicate balance of the local economy.

OWAIN: So in we go.

(Sounds of Afghanistan: heat, streets, markets, beggars)

Kabul, the Afghan capital, is kinda like the Sennybridge training range, but without a sewage system.
Rusting shells of tanks. Two-dimensional buildings with whole families sleeping in 'em. Not roads, just tracks; kids playing in ditches next to lumps of twisted metal and human shit.
We make the connection with the salesmen in a hotel.
Three lads from Maidstone, Stockport and Aberdeen.
Nervous as fuck.

IESTYN: Remember: 'We are not here to fight anyone.
Just to keep the clients safe'.

CAI: While we sniff around.

IESTYN: We take the following day to plan the route,
then leave the city gate by Night.
We take the boys to a secret lab up in the hills.
(*Assuming formation*)
I drive the first 4x4: reconnaissance.

OWAIN: (*Assuming formation*)
I take the middle one, with the jittery salesmen.

CAI: (*Assuming formation*)
I'm in backup position, look-out for any rear attack.

IESTYN: We come to an outcrop of old brick buildings.
They look designed for storage, not habitation. Deserted.

(disembarking and investigating)

OWAIN: Inside one, there's a trap door to a cellar:
where we find two young Afghan lads –
(Sonic change: underground lab) - with a filtration system.

CAI: Then the whole place shakes.
clumps of dust fall out the ceiling.

(They cower: Explosion)

IESTYN: Mortar fire!

OWAIN: Military, not bandits.

CAI: Then quiet. Letting us stew.

OWAIN: An' the salesmen ARE stewing: so's you can smell em.

IESTYN: The two Afghan boys have pistols.

CAI: We have foldaway AK machine guns.

OWAIN: We ask the Afghans if they're expectin' company.

IESTYN: They mutter something. They speak two English words we don't understand at first.

OWAIN: We catch them second time round:

CAI: 'Land-lord'; 'Rent'.
They're behind with their payments.
That's why the mortar shells are
knocking on the door.

IESTYN: They'll have seen our vehicles.

OWAIN: They'll expect at least three visitors.

CAI: We tell the Afghan boys: invite the 'landlords' in.

OWAIN: We fold up the AKs into the canvas bags we carry.

IESTYN: Two men come in, wearing ski-masks, carrying semi-automatic weapons.

CAI: Blue eyes, both.

IESTYN: They tell the Afghans to turn over the money they

were going to give the salesmen.
These men have English accents.

OWAIN: Cai strikes up conversation.

CAI: We're in security. We believe in economic growth.

OWAIN: The sight of the money makes one of them relax,
get a bit cocky. He says 'We came. We saw.
We fracked'.
Cai grins.

CAI: Right, then. Frack this -

OWAIN: Cai's wearin' a glove, holding this vial of clear
liquid that he's palmed from the lab.
He breaks an' throws it into those blue eyes –

CAI: Which steam an' blister into bubbles,
as the screaming starts –

IESTYN: The Esperanto of Pain!

OWAIN: Screams from the skeleton teeth of burnt off lips –

CAI: We dive for the AKs in our bags –

IESTYN: Find 'em, twist an' roll, aim –

(Machine gun fire)

OWAIN: It's over in four seconds flat.

IESTYN: *(Triumphantly)* PLISMONA BRO!!

CAI: *("Helpful" translation:)* 'Neighbourhood Policing'. *(Beat)* One of the salesmen has fainted –

IESTYN: Smells like his mates need their nappies changed.

CAI: Check the damage.

OWAIN: Fuckin' hell. I have just shot a Brit.
A fucking British soldier.

IESTYN: Off duty. Way off-duty.

OWAIN: But British soldiers. Christ, lads.
This'll take some explaining.

CAI: We'll sort it.

IESTYN: We sort things.

CAI: We'll say we charged them with 'Aggravated trespass'.

(A door slams, in a deadened space:
Together in a particularly cheerless hotel room)

OWAIN: Back in the hotel, there are no drinks.

IESTYN: No spliffs.

OWAIN: I keep thinking about the dead Brits.
So we wind down by telling stories.

IESTYN: You know what I thought of, tonight? 3am,
Salisbury Plain. Song o' the birds. Whipperwhill.
Bittern. In the thorn bushes. *(Beat)*
No birdsong here.

OWAIN: I know that. The quiet, just before the training
exercise starts. Then orange lights and CS gas.
Fifty men in respirators, moving like a wave.
The men we shot:
would have done those exercises, too.

CAI: Hey, it's Saturday night. Woss your favourite music,
of a Saturday night?

OWAIN: Oh, a bit of AC/DC. 'I'm on the Highway to Hell' –

CAI: Iestyn? C'mon, Saturday night: that's a piece o'
British culture worth fightin' for.

IESTYN: T. REX.

CAI: WHAT?

IESTYN: T. FUCKIN' REX, mun. The sly, hipswinging, anthems of the wild groover.

OWAIN: That mean fuck all.

IESTYN: Hymns to the flared nostril.
The sweet perfume of the dirt.

CAI: Y'know what T. FUCKING REX sound like to ME? A SHEEP whose exposed brain has been chewed by crows, tryin' to BLEAT a nursery rhyme. To some elves'n'fairies. Who 'ave been made paraplegic by some toxic joss sticks. Which this Addled Sheep has then STUCK UP ITS NOSE. *(Beat)* More like. TRY HARDER!

IESTYN: No, it sets me up for a Saturday night, hunting the scent of a woman who's wetter
than an otter's pocket.

CAI: It sets you up as a sad puppet.
With a scrotum fulla SAWDUST.

IESTYN: That attitude is just FUCKING TYPICAL.

It's how most people make –
anythin' EXPERIMENTAL –
seem LAUGHABLE an' ridiculous.
Y'know, your objection to T. Rex is purely on the grounds of fashion. I hate fashion.
It is an industry which takes the changin' cycles of the seasons, an' makes it into somethin' bitchy an' shallow. Seasons are somethin' as was meant to tell us about the deeper friction, of man in the universe.

CAI: So for you, T. cowin' Rex
speaks of the 'deeper friction of man',
in the fuckin' 'universe' - ?

IESTYN: Aye, it does.
The infinite promise of that very thing.
That WHIFF of combined attraction AND antagonism. From which, we LEARN.

CAI: Shit an' piss.

OWAIN: OK, change the subject.
Think of a place, where you'd like to be. *(Pause)*

CAI: A high rock. Sandstone. Looking down from a cliff.
To the sea. A beach, with pools. Sun setting.
(Pause)

IESTYN: Early morning arrival in a European city.
After a train journey, overnight.
Lucerne. Rome. Heat of the day just starting.
A chair in a cream coloured plaza. Fountain spray.
(Pause)

OWAIN: I don't know. Anywhere.
With a clean cut victory. Can't see it. *(Beat.)*
Can't see it. *(Beat.)*
And we head back. To debrief an' report.
MI6 HQ. Two fatalities, sir.
British army personnel: who had gone rogue.
Are we covered?

CHIEF: Standard line.
Victims of a ruthless Taliban ambush.
Died protecting bystander civilians from the
firefight. You three are, to all intents and
purposes, in the pay of a private security firm.
So no disciplinary procedures,
no follow-up paperwork.

OWAIN: No comeback? At all?

CHIEF: Ex-corporal Wright will tell you,
no Bloody Sunday enquiry would ever
satisfy both sides. Probably neither.
We learnt from that experience.

Your tracks are covered.

OWAIN: So: out there, 'to all intents and purposes' –
we're above the law?

CHIEF: While you don't claim military status.
You're private sector workers,
in a responsive industry. How was Thomas?

OWAIN: He was *(beat)* effective.
He and Wright were a tight team. I'm surprised
Wright's the one who's flagging up concerns about
Thomas. Strikes me, it'd be the other way round.
Wright's the one who seems less screwed-on.

CHIEF: So what is Thomas screwing down on, so tight?

OWAIN: I dunno. Himself, I s'pose.

CHIEF: Find out his contents. Any harmful additives. *(Beat)*
Your next destination is Iraq. Baghdad.
The situation there is different.
There's some legislation in place.
If you gun down civilians in the street, you
might just about be prosecuted under US law.
But we're expecting you to show SOME discretion.

OWAIN: Yes, sir.

CHIEF: You're signed up with a new American firm.
It's won the contract from the US government,
to pick up the reins, redevelop the water and
sewage system. One third of the funding for this
sort of redevelopment in Baghdad gets spent on
commercial security. But there's value-added if the
firm can show it's putting money into the local
economy: like, hiring and training local Iraqi
ex-soldiers as manpower for the security patrols.
If they shape up, you give them a badge, a uniform
and a sense of pride. That's your cover.
So: get over there; and help keep the peace.

OWAIN: Yes, sir.
(*On the plane: with CAI*)
Where's Iestyn?

CAI: 'E was out on the piss, last night.

OWAIN: So what's it like?

IESTYN: *(suddenly arriving, still pissed*
and detectably marinating)
Iraq is, in many ways, like being shoved off
a diving board, into a seething volcano.
Inside of this, is a cathedral of debris, irrigated
by infectious sewage.
Walk through its door, you drop down

and land on a sort of maddening
bouncy-castle-labyrinth,
which is laced with razorwire.
And I said, after the last time, I would definitely:
DO IT AGAIN!!
I often feel rampant when I'm still wrecked
from the night before.
Then I wake up, and start feelin' tired.

CAI: Go to sleep an' sober up.

IESTYN: *(Sudden comedown)* 'Ere, Cai.
How'd I get from there to 'ere?

CAI: *(Briefly nonplussed)* On this PLANE, you prat.

IESTYN: No, no. I mean. THERE.
You know. I was in Belfast in the 80s.
From THERE to here?
We knew the enemy, even if we was losing.
Still felt there was something worth fighting for.
But now, what is it? EXACTLY?

CAI: Yer talking shite. *(They land, with a few bumps.)*

IESTYN: No, I'm not. I know. I know that,
only when people feel they are defendin' something,
will they UNITE.

OWAIN: An', we're in Military Intelligence.
With responsibility for Defence.

IESTYN: No, this is security. Security ain't defence.
And it ain't Intelligence.

OWAIN: What the fuck?

IESTYN: But nowadays, they're sayin', security's better
than money, better than sex, better than water.
Not freedom to do things – freedom from things.
(Beat) Look at it long enough, it's almost -
(a burst of revelation) BUDDHIST.

OWAIN: Security's a natural right, Iest.
People want freedom from what threatens 'em,
invades their space –

IESTYN: Yes, mun.
The room in which they store their THINGS.
Not people, THINGS.
The room where they wanna stay quietly,
with their THINGS.

CAI: Bollocks.

IESTYN: That's just you. Allus IN DENIAL.
The man in denial. Is the one.
Who is skatin', on the ice of hopelessness.
Like a HOT PENGUIN.

(Sounds of Baghdad: heat, insects,
a hot outside yard)

OWAIN: Iestyn gets his mojo back when he's rehydrated an' had some sleep. He cheers himself up by plannin' to teach the local Iraqi volunteers to sing 'Land of My Fathers',
an' tellin' 'em it's the English national anthem.

CAI: We employ former soldiers whenever we can.
Sworn enemies of the coalition ten years ago.
Plus some taxi drivers.
Farmers who've owned a rifle but never used one.
Kurds, Christians, other Iraqi minorities -

IESTYN: They look good in their uniforms.

CAI: We treat 'em fair.

OWAIN: We give 'em a name. The Red Dragons.

IESTYN: We set up a scramble drill for crisis situations.
We lead the team through this drill every five days.

OWAIN: We tell them. *(To audience)*
We ain't paid to kill people. We get paid to
save lives, and minimize any trouble.
We 're facilitators: makin' sure, the proper
water and sewage facilities get built.
That's gotta be good for everyone.

CAI: But if anyone STARTS 'any trouble',
we're ready to 'outsource' that trouble.
Right back up their arse.

IESTYN: We are the outsorcerers. Teachin'
YOU how to do it.

OWAIN: How to do what we do back home.
We're just trainin' staff, further afield.

CAI: Good land with natural resources will always
be valued. 'Specially with low corporate tax rates.

IESTYN: That ain't a loophole in the system.
It IS the system. Always has been.

CAI: The British Empire is a thing of the past.
We've ditched it.
We are not occupiers: we are liberators.
Safeguarding YOUR national assets and people.

OWAIN: We focus on creating jobs and wealth elsewhere.

IESTYN: We work like fathers,
who pass the knowledge on to their sons.

OWAIN: We are rebuilding Iraq.
Offering increased security to you, the Iraqis.

IESTYN: An' we will teach you, how we revive our spirits
with a rendition of our national anthem.

OWAIN: C'mon, Cai. It'll do yer heart good to hear
the Red Dragons give it their all.

CAI: Well, there's enough of 'em ter make a racket.

IESTYN: Which is the first step to righteous passion.
C'mon, Owain, join in.

OWAIN: Right enough. We give 'em the title,
the North East Baghdad Male Voice Choir.

IESTYN: Every morning I will say to you,
'Who are you boys?'
An' you answer back:
'We are the North East Baghdad Male Voice Choir'.
Then I ask: 'An' WHAT are you?'
An' you reply: 'We are Full of Eastern Promise'.

OWAIN: Which is a line from an ancient heroic myth.

IESTYN: Here we go.

(OWAIN and CAI begin to sing the proper song, but rapidly fade out as they hear what IESTYN is in fact singing: Nigel Jenkins's parody version)

IESTYN: My hen laid a haddock, one hand oiled a flea,
Glad farts and centurions threw dogs in the sea,
I could stew a hare here and brandish Dan's flan,
Don's ruddy bog's blocked up with sand.
(*Chorus: in which OWAIN and CAI join as best they can*)
Dad! Dad! Why don't you oil Auntie Glad?
Can whores appear in beer bottle pies,
O butter the hens as they fly!

CAI: Iest. Iest. What in the name of God's almighty Arse was that?

OWAIN: That's a fucking PARODY, mun.

IESTYN: Yes, course I know that.
But, see lads, my Welsh ain't actually that good.
So I got my iphone an' went on Wikipedia
to find the song lyrics.

I found that version by this bloke Nigel Jenkins,
which I thought would be easier for me to remember,
an' easier for the raghead bobtails to learn.
It's workin' a treat. They don't 'alf give it some.
When they put some vibrato on the top notes,
it's like they're callin' the faithful to prayer.

CAI: So every fuckin' morning: we will be teachin'
fifty Iraqis: who for all we know might be
blackmailed to be wired up as suicide bombers,
an' take us out: to sing about stewin' hares, brandishin'
flans, an' oiling their Aunty Fuckin' Glad?

IESTYN: Yeah. But when they don't crack a smile – it's kinda
moving. They've already got it down better than
John Redwood. I think it bucks 'em up a bit, the singin'.
(They look out, around them. Beat. We switch to private downtime, back in the cheerless hotel)

OWAIN: Some of these local boys are pretty good shots.

CAI: That's the military training.

OWAIN: They seem keen. Ter get involved.

CAI: Yeah. Well, it's work. Hard to come by since 2003.
That's when, this American bloke Paul Bremer,
gets put in charge of reconstruction. Bremer
disbands the Iraqi army, and their police force.

IESTYN: Suddenly, half a million armed men.
Out on the streets. Only two ways
for them to get money: join the insurgents;
or organized crime.

CAI: Bremer claims there's no viable Iraqi security
infrastructure. An' there ain't,
now he's got rid of the local army and police.
An' put American troops in charge.

IESTYN: Before Saddam was toppled, he set up training
in guerrilla warfare.
Now the unemployed arm themselves
from ammunition dumps: arsenals
that 'ave been hidden all over the country.
That's wot yer call 'transferable skills'.

OWAIN: Bloody hell.

CAI: It gets worse. Bremer sacks anyone who was
part of Saddam's ruling Ba'ath party, saying
this'll get rid of the corruption of the old regime.
But there were no other no other political parties,
in existence.
You had to be a member of the Ba'ath party to
get anywhere, or hold down a job, in a government
office, hospital, school, university, anywhere.
So there's another 50,000 skilled, intelligent,

middle classes, an' thousands of teachers
– without work.

IESTYN: The government buildings get bombed out.
Schools and hospitals are looted and burned.

CAI: Families an' dependents.
Discoverin' 'freedom and democracy'.
They get pissed off. Specially the youngsters.
How'd YOU feel?

OWAIN: *(Beat)* Probably - pissed off.

CAI: No electricity or water. Shit running in the streets.
Gangs take charge. Gangs that steal an' rape an'
kidnap. For ransom.

IESTYN: At least: in Northern Ireland, we tried to make sure
we only pissed off the CATHOLICS.

CAI: It's gone lawless.
So: think of it as a Western, an' we're the sheriffs.

IESTYN: That's what the Yanks do.

CAI: Problem is, many Muslims over in Saudi Arabia,
an' Syria, an' Yemen an' Egypt see it like the
Spanish Civil War. An honourable cause.

IESTYN: Which they can join by riggin' IEDs
and land mines

CAI: Join the jihad. Escape poverty.
Make your family proud. Holy War.
Connect yourself forever with the bravest and best
in the traditions of your land. Your fathers.
In their situation: wouldn't you do the same?

OWAIN: But. I. Am. Not. In. Their. Situation.

CAI: Course you're not.
Nobody could be arsed to seriously fuck up
the native infrastructure and resources of Wales,
would they?

IESTYN: 'Cos we haven't got any.

CAI: Not any more.

OWAIN: Wales never had any 'weapons of mass destruction'

CAI: Yeah, well, they didn't find any here either. India,
Pakistan, North Korea, or Israel, yes.
Mind you, Bremer said one shrewd thing.

OWAIN: Woss that then?

CAI: He said: 'If you don't know what you stand for;
you cannot easily figure out how to defend it'.
Thass wot gives the jihadis: the edge.
Unless we find: a sharper edge than them.

*(MASSIVE SHUDDERING EXPLOSION
AND LOSS OF LIGHT: CAI AND IESTYN
SWITCH ON TORCHES)*

CAI: I'll check downstairs *(scrambles away)*.

IESTYN: *(in an intent whisper)* I told you, he's Been Turned.
He's right inside the jihadi mindset.

OWAIN: 'Ang on, isn't he just tryin' to size up the situation
an' know the enemy?
We gotta know the lie of the land.
You just said, this AIN'T like Northern Ireland –

IESTYN: No it ain't, but I don't go sayin',
'In their situation: wouldn't you do the same?'–

OWAIN: But don't you 'AVE to do that?
Get inside the enemy: know their motives,
guess their tactics?

IESTYN: Al Qaeda an' Isis are the enemies, not the Iraqis.
That's crucial.

OWAIN: Sure. But we have to have a sense of what might make the Iraqis go over to Al Qaeda an' Isis, an' suddenly stab us in the backs.

IESTYN: I woudn't put it past Thomas. Ter start the stabbin'. Hold the camera for an Isis video. Starrin' us.

OWAIN: Fuckin' hell, Iest.
You an' Cai have been through hell an' high water –

IESTYN: We have been tried, an' we 'ave been tested.
An' we have always COME THROUGH.
That matters to me.
Owain: my father was a soldier.
My grandfather was a soldier.
An' my great-grandfather was a soldier.
An' sometimes it is an awful job.
Sometimes it turns yer stomach, an' it makes you puke. But it is necessary.
Because it is necessary, it has morality.
And because it has morality, it has dignity.
If we prove equal to the challenge:
we earn the right to be among the best of men.
We prove to be a warrior: unselfish an' TRUE.
What would I say to my father and grandfather and great-grandfather if I couldn't?
I will not break rank.

But Thomas: he is not a true warrior.
He has let his life TWIST his sense of purpose;
and an' his sense of loyalty. That's a weakness.
An' it will be fatal to us. Unless we do something.

OWAIN: What?

IESTYN: Confront him. Interrogate him.

OWAIN: Iestyn, we are losin' the big picture.

IESTYN: What big picture? Whose big picture?

OWAIN: Look, mun.
The world we're being told to build doesn't make sense. Any more than the world we were born into.
Unless we force it to.

IESTYN: We ARE forcin' it to.

OWAIN: Maybe you are forcin' it a bit too hard.
Like a fugitive turd.

IESTYN: My turds are not fugitives. *(Beat)*
Fugitives from what?

OWAIN: Yourself.

IESTYN: Myself? How can something actually INSIDE OF me, be a fugitive, FROM MYSELF?

OWAIN: Fuckin' 'ell, mun, we 'ave all had times when we need ter pass a turd an'can't.
An' there are other situations, I 'ave known an' observed. When a fear, LEADS to its own confirmation. *(Beat)* I call it: *(Beat)*
The Minotaur of Anticipation.
Squattin' in the Maze of Logic.

IESTYN: You what?

OWAIN: You heard. The Minotaur of Anticipation;
Squattin' in the Maze of Logic.

IESTYN: Yes, I 'ave heard it, an' I'm still tryin' to get my head around it.

OWAIN: Of course you are.
But you can't, see? Thass the point.
Still: you can VISUALIZE the Minotaur.
Can't you? Squattin' in the Maze.

IESTYN: Er – yeah – yeah, I can –

OWAIN: But you can't get your head around it.

Jesus, who the fuck can GET their HEAD –
physically I mean - AROUND A FUCKIN'
MINOTAUR?
Can't be done. *(Beat)*
That's the point.

IESTYN: Right. So. *(Beat)* What DO we do, then?

OWAIN: We keep calm, an' carry on.
Like it says on them posters an' coffee mugs an' –
tea towels.

IESTYN: Right. Tea towels.

OWAIN: Tea towels. NOT Minotaurs.

IESTYN: Right. *(Lights up. CAI re-enters)*

CAI: Insurgents blew up the water pipeline.
They thought it was oil. Shorted the electricity.
Two sentries dead in the blast. Pity.
They wuz two of the best tenors in the morning choir.

OWAIN: Aw, what?

CAI: Now, what used ter be their insides, are all over
our fuckin' Humvee. Great soggy red pile o' meat
sat on the windscreen.

I've asked their mates to hose it down.
Then notify the families.
But the stink is gonna linger.

OWAIN: They okay? 'Bout doin' that?

CAI: Yeah. The town's quiet.
Under Saddam, people sometimes used to go out in couples or families. See friends, go to a restaurant.
Now everyone stays indoors, all the time.
'Cept the gangs.

(They start the motions of bedding down.)

OWAIN: We try for sleep. You writhe around for ages;
then it swallows you up.

(They do so, for six seconds.
Then, snap into: a suddenly arrived Morning)

IESTYN: *(oppressively cheerful)*
It'll take more than wot happened last night to put me down.
A Pro-Plus tablet; stick my head under a tap;
an' I'm the real deal again.
Hey, lads, when we meet our local team this morning:
let's give 'em a little somethin' extra.
Raise all of our spirits. Turn our spunk to steel.

OWAIN: You keep clear of anythin' ter do with my spunk.

IESTYN: The proper response to crisis, is ter be INVENTIVE.

(He draws the other two into a murmuring planning huddle. After quick negotiations, their visible scepticism is overcome by IESTYN'S sheer force of insistence. They assemble, smiling, before the audience, who stand in for the local volunteers, assembled outside the building. A hot space: an outdoors yard)

Lads. Or, as we say in Wales, *Meibion*.
That is you: *Meibion* Baghdad.
We depend on you. You keep us all safe: together.
One day your land WILL be calm an' peaceful again.
In the meantime, we do what we have to.
And, forged fast by the heat of our special misery,
we will stand proud at the end.
It will have made us: who we are.
An' one day, when this is all over:
we will be able to welcome you:
as brothers, to our land.
So you can see where WE came from.
The beauty, we stand up for.
That time and space: of peace. Lost, and yet to come.
We won't die. We CAN'T die. Until we –
RECAPTURE – that sense of beauty in the world.
There are wonderful things. Out there.

You have to make it THROUGH these awful times;
an' stay alive ter see them.
Together; with us. For your steadfast courage
in the face of enemy fire: this morning I respectfully
dedicate to YOU: this hymn of praise.
To OUR homeland. That, one day - far away from all this
– will open up: to YOU.

(They set up a rhythm, stamping and clapping, and IESTYN takes the lead, to the tune of Bachman-Turner Overdrive's 'You Ain't Seen Nothin' Yet'. Note: revised lyrics developed from an original idea by Russ Gomer/David Garland Jones, with his knowledge and permission.)

Sun rise on Aberystwyth
And on Newport down in Gwent
Bandit plains of wild Tregaron (*one whistles the riff from Morricone's 'The Good, The Bad and the Ugly'*)
And Dolgellau's dark intent

Now we're shittin' bricks in Baghdad
And we sure could use a lift, so this is Iestyn's gift,
Put yer fist around yer manhood, becaauuuse
You ain't seen Ruthin yet
Don't fuss with Ffairfach, cos you ain't seen Ruthin yet
It's somethin', it's somethin',
you ain't never ever gonna forget
Turn down Tredegar, cos you ain't seen Ruthin yet

The green pastures of Llangefni
The musky whiff of Wrexham town
Cosmopolitan Porthmadog
And Mwnt, the jewel in Cardi's crown,
Mwnt repelled Flemish invaders
Now their bones adorn the shore
(they ain't comin' back for more)
Hit the high trail down through Trefnant, becaauuuuse
You ain't seen Ruthin yet
S-s-s-skip Sketty, cos you ain't seen Ruthin yet
It's somethin', it's somethin',
you ain't never ever gonna forget
LLLLlet go Llandrindod, cos you ain't seen Ruthin yet

(*more assorted feral ad-libs*)

The hormones motor in Machynlleth
The craic and banter of Crickhowell
Famous warriors of Cilmery
Will never once throw in the towel

We got our own Valhalla
That red fort nestlin' by the Clwyd
Where the heroes spill their fluid *(mimes wanking)*
There's a printer's press on Well Street
Yes sir,
You ain't seen Ruthin yet

Tremblin' in Emlyn, cos they ain't seen Ruthin yet
It's somethin', it's somethin', you ain't never ever gonna forget! F-f-f-fade away Fishguard,
cos you ain't seen Ruthin yet

No, you ain't seen Ruthin YET!!

(Pause to regain breath.)

CAI: I think they liked that.

OWAIN: Yeah, good one, Iest.

IESTYN: Went well. They didn't actually know the places.
Or even, really, understand what we were singin' about.
But they responded. They got INTO it.

OWAIN: I think they picked up on the FEELING we were puttin' into the words. Even though they weren't dead serious.
I mean, we wuz sendin' it up, with the place names, 'avin' a laugh, an' then I thought, dammit – I really wanna SEE DOLGELLAU. Never thought I'd SAY that. All that dingy vertical slate, pubs seethin' with beer an' resentment, bottled up: where all you can do is hammer down the pints.
An afternoon in Ruthin would actually be - great.
The castle, an' the clock Tower. Even Siop Nain.
Fuck, I could even get off on an hour in Anglesey…

CAI: The smell of a Clark's pie when you leave the pub.

IESTYN: Tom Jones on the jukebox.
Women with sly but generous smiles, that say 'yes'.

OWAIN: Catatonia singin' 'Shore Leave'.

CAI: The Manics…
(Sound of a mobile phone; CAI answers)
Hello? Yeh … *(goes aside to converse)*

OWAIN: 'Stead of heat and flies, and sewage in the streets.

IESTYN: Listen. I got the word. Last night I got a text
from an informant. Local intel, like back in Belfast.
He reckons Thomas will make contact with an
insurgent cell tonight.
This is it. When we give him enough rope.
We follow him.
And, if we get the evidence,
we are prepared to take him out.

OWAIN: Take him OUT?
I thought you said confront him –
an' interrogate him.

IESTYN: We might not have the chance.
To take him alive for questioning.

OWAIN: Take him OUT? Jesus. *(Beat)*
That would make us even more – isolated.

IESTYN: We have each other, to watch our backs. *(Beat)*
With the volunteers, the trick is to act like nothin' surprises us, we anticipated anythin' that happens. Everythin' confirms us further in what we are doin'. No turning back. Our faith: is what inspires faith, and commands loyalty. In them.

OWAIN: Faith in what?

IESTYN: (*snaps back like a rifle bolt*)
Our purpose, you cunt. Never lose your grip.
Remember, we say, we are contractors;
but we are better than contractors.
They serve money, not their country.
And we are better than soldiers, who are trained to implement orders, but not to imagine.
We are intelligence, with purpose.
Cementing us together. Depending on each other.
You will NOT bottle out now.
You are not ALLOWED. It is NOT
JUST about YOU.
I need to know I can TRUST you,

in order to do what I have to do. And you me.
Now, do you trust me?

OWAIN: Yes.

IESTYN: Owain, this is the ultimate test:
the one you have actually been seeking since you
joined up. You gotta discover yer EVIL, enough
EVIL ter hold yerself together. *(CAI re-enters)*

CAI: I've got the word.
Those who triggered the blast are hidin' up in the hills.
I've directions to the house.
So we're goin' up there, after them. Right now.

OWAIN: Could be a trap.

CAI: Could be a trap.

IESTYN: So we trap the trappers. Up for it.

OWAIN: UP for it.
(Subtle underscore: an electric simmering)

CAI: Comin' for them.

IESTYN: Bringin' it on.

OWAIN: Bringin' the hell.

CAI: Spreadin' it around, chasin' it back,
to where it needs to go.

OWAIN: To those who've deserved it.

IESTYN: Those who taunt us.

CAI: Those who question our faith.

IESTYN: Fuck work and safety. Time for play and danger.

CAI: We tell our enemies:
we have bullets which we want to GIVE
(generous smile) you.
They are what you NEED; to lodge just there,
an' there, an' there, inside your body.
An' make it perfect.

OWAIN: We are the quick; an' they are the dead.

CAI: We make friends with Death.
We extend it to those we meet. That thing waiting
inside us all. Unstoppable.
We work with it, to speed up the process.
The deathspeed.
That's us.

IESTYN: We are coming for you.
We are the righteous, hunting you down,
to render you down.

CAI: Spring the cages. Release the madness.
Bathe in it, taste it, embrace it, kiss it,
swallow it, force it, wear it, become it.
We are Havoc.

IESTYN: We're on our way to find you out.

Fast L/X fade, to Interval

S/X: 'Written on the Forehead' by P. J. Harvey,
from the cd Let England Shake.

Part Two

Cave scene: The Company: Huw Blainey as Cai. Photos by Keith Morris.

(Desert wind of the hills above Baghdad.)

CAI: We trek to the foothills, outside Baghdad.
Our night vision lenses scan for human heat.

IESTYN: Where everything else has been blasted to sand.

OWAIN: Sand that's been blasted to grinning hate.
Waiting to jump up and leer at you.

CAI: Hunting human heat. That shows up, as a sucking wound of light.

IESTYN: We've brought two of the volunteers,
who know the terrain.

OWAIN: It's like the boulders are humming somethin' to each other. Somethin', we can't even imagine.
We're playing chess with something
We don't know what it is –

IESTYN: But we will find out
And we will beat it
One way or another.

OWAIN: Clambering up a hill of sand.
It starts to feel like sloping mash of squelching jellyfish.
Oozing death -

IESTYN: Turning your entrails to shit -

OWAIN: There's a broken building.
Like a bonewhite skull: dead-eyed. Shepherd's croft.
Abandoned. Or rigged for an ambush?

IESTYN: We fan out. I go right, in an arc, like I'm goin' round; but I'm checkin' the side windows.

OWAIN: I take the left. I see a small back yard, and outhouse.

IESTYN: I take one of our local guides, Ahmed. He is forty-five, with a family to feed, and desperate for work since he lost his job for belonging to the Ba'ath party.

OWAIN: With me goes Saeed. He has a lazy eye and a filthy grin, so I call him Jack Elam.

CAI: I walk forward, an' I do what I do in combat situations.
I call up the spectral double which the Egyptians named the Ka: the male spirit.
When you let the Ka spirit take you over,
he directs your movements and puts you in the flow.
This involves the opposite of fear.
The blind dog of Mortality sniffs out fear.
The blind dog of Mortality has a broken skull
and an exposed brain: panting and slavering.
If he bites you, you go blind like him.

This lets in fear, makes you weak.
When you merge with the Ka spirit, an' put him in charge, he can see the dog, and see what the dog cannot see. Now you have the advantage.

OWAIN: I think, what the fuck is Cai doin'?

CAI: Weak men let the male spirit of the KA get confused, and replaced, with the motorized body container of their fuckin' CAR: in which they place their daft faith, and submit to the one way system.
In a situation like this, Jeremy Cunting Clarkson would stand exposed an' goose-pimply as what he is: an XXL Shopping Bag of Wank.You tell the spirit:
I do not give myself to rage without cause.
An' it slows the time around you.
So you can home in.

IESTYN: Is he trying to draw fire?

CAI: I am parting the fear. Gliding up through it.
You basically treat every moment like it is great sex.
Sex without fear feeds the spirit.
You see and feel yourself somersaulting forwards out of the limits of being human.
Everything in your slipstream is now drawn in, working to help you, and sending back the hatred flung in your direction, with double force.

So the faster you put things behind you, the better.
I run at the door, aiming myself, not at it,
but three metres behind it.

OWAIN: MUZZLE FLASH, WINDOW ABOVE!

IESTYN: AK47 primed –

OWAIN: AK47 primed –

CAI: Roll in low past the kicked-in door, snap out AK47,
riddle the ceiling of the ground floor room.
They scream, upstairs.

OWAIN: I sprint for the cover of the outhouse. Saeed has locked up with fear.

IESTYN: I shoot at the top side window.

OWAIN: Saeed unsticks; he runs across the yard towards me.

IESTYN: I sprint round the right side, to the back of the outhouse,
hopin' Ahmed will follow me.

OWAIN: The back door is open, an' the stairwell faces out.
Something bounces down the stairs,
dangerously light and round –

CAI: I hear it coming, breathe in
and kick it out the back door –

OWAIN: Detonation

IESTYN: Detonation

OWAIN: Hissing fog engulfs Saeed

IESTYN: Chlorine gas -

OWAIN: CHLORINE GAS –

IESTYN: We've no masks –

CAI: I mount the stairwell. Move deep an' coiled, not high
an' rigid. Can't let them fire another gas grenade.
In case they have another ready, I send up my spirit,
ahead of my physical body, to detonate it in their belt.
No explosion, so they DON'T have another.
That will make it easier for me. Their desperation.
Which I breathe down, draw deep into me.
Their fear pumps my blood: stronger.

OWAIN: I find my EpiPen injector.
This will give me one dose of Epinephrine, help
me withstand the gas.
I jam it in the muscle of my outer mid-thigh.

IESTYN: I find mine and do the same. We've one apiece.
None spare for Saeed or Ahmed.

OWAIN: I watch Saeed trying to cough out his burning
lungs. I tell myself chlorine gas is rarely fatal.
He will probably survive. It provokes panic and
trauma; but is ineffective as a weapon of death.
In most cases.

CAI: I catapult myself out the downstairs room,
put the gas behind me, an' rush up the stairs,
firing. The approaching smell of fear and anger is too
powerful for one man.
There are two. I listen for their heat.

IESTYN: I take a big, lungbusting chest of air and dash
across the yard. On the heels of a Thomas,
like BACK IN BELFAST!
But THIS time, we shall WIN.
At WHATEVER the cost. Nothing Will stop us.

CAI: I hear stumbling movement round the left corner
of the stairwell top. I pick that one 'cos he'll be
off balance. My spirit sees his death as an already
accomplished fact. I give it to him, as a gift.
My bullets release him: from his past
and his present and his future.

IESTYN: The second insurgent jumps out the right-hand room, steadies his gun 'gainst the wall of the landing, aiming to shoot Cai in the back.
He turns his head at the neck, an' sees me at the foot of the stairs: too late. His rifle moves slower than his eyes. My shots whack him against the wall, an' burst his brain to pebbledash.
Most expensive form of decoration known to man.
Or, maybe: the cheapest.

OWAIN: The gas scatters, in a sharp night wind.
I give Saeed my water to try and help his coughing and moaning, as he rocks back and forth like a kid.
Ahmed looks on, not knowing what to do.
In the sudden silence, he laughs,
like an imploding hoover.

CAI: We reload. Then secure the rooms.

IESTYN: Check for IEDs.

CAI: Collect the weapons.

IESTYN: Find a dozen brick-sized chunks of C-4 plastic explosive. And a car battery.
These boys caused last night's explosion.

CAI: Or else they were plannin' somethin' very similar.

OWAIN: Now the EpiPen is kicking in, my blood is racin' high. When this stuff's in your system,
you can fight on, foaming with fury till you're a limbless trunk, and even then you'll bite through boots. But I feel I oughta stay with Saeed.
His coughs are subsiding.
Shit, I feel like I could run up a wall an' across the ceiling. Even though I'm outdoors. I spot a desert hedgehog, peering out from a rock, an' have An Amazin' Idea. We could strap explosives
to this desert hedgehog.
We could name it Bastion. Bastion the Wonder Hedgehog, trained to navigate or detonate IEDs, and then, if still INTACT, shuffle into insurgents' camps on a suicide mission: stupidly intrepid or intrepidly stupid, OR BOTH AT THE SAME TIME! GO ON YOU BASTION, KAMIKAZE HEDGEHOG, HONOUR YOUR FATHERS AN' SCORE FOR WALES! MANY PRICKLY VIRGINS AWAIT YOUR HEROIC POSTHUMOUS COCK!

CAI: You what?

OWAIN: Nuthin', I think I'm, er, startin' to trip out a bit on the EpiPen.

IESTYN: Me too.

OWAIN: Ahmed is lookin' strangely attractive.
Wall-eyed an' hairy an' yet – seductive…
What about Saeed? We can't just leave him.

CAI: Owain: we protect the right things and people.
Everything else: we speed up the natural process.
Ahmed can take Saeed back to his home. They can curse his luck together, in their own language.
It'll be good for both of 'em, sharin' that moment, with one of their own.

OWAIN: *(simultaneously dazed, hyper, trippy)*
The 'right things and people'.
Hey, lads! *(sincere curiosity, not rhetoric)*
Whatd'ya reckon they ARE?

IESTYN: Yer shittin' through yer mouth.
We know the WRONG people.
They are not freedom fighters, they are deathbound fanatics fixin' to die an' kill in jihad.
They want to replace the civilization an' culture of centuries with their rule of law.
No rights, no blessings: count your duties.
We saw that in Afghanistan under the Taliban.

OWAIN: Yeah. But what if the Iraqis feel like they're caught in a war between two asset-strippers?
How many 'rights or blessings' left for them?
We're "keeping Britain safe", right?
All we've done since we've been here is behave like the security contractors,
what we're pretendin' to be.

IESTYN: We are here to foil the enemy's plans.
In war, that involves giving the enemy a precisely focussed show of the ruthlessness and violence of which we are capable: in order to break his will; in the shortest time possible.
That is what we do. It is the least wrong thing to do. If we did nothing, it would be worse.
The will of the enemy would be unchecked.

CAI: Look. Maybe they wanted to lure us out of the town. There could be an ambush, closin' around us, in a horseshoe.

IESTYN: So let's get back to town.

CAI: NO. Let's go further up into the hills.

IESTYN: Yer what?

CAI: Last thing they'll expect.

OWAIN: Ahmed and Saeed –

CAI: Can always give away our whereabouts or be tortured till they do.
Common sense suggests we'll be following behind them. So we do the opposite.
Uncommon sense.

IESTYN: *(After a pause)* All right.

OWAIN: Where is Cai taking us?
Then I get it: I owe him my life. I'm only breathin' and thinkin' right now 'cos he ran up an' took out those insurgents.
Shit, the epinephrine is makin' my heartbeat a jackhammer, an' it will be takin' Iestyn the same road any minute – then I see it happen.
Iestyn kicks off: starts jumpin' on the insurgents' corpses, to burst their heads -

IESTYN: Fuckin' bastards! Fuckin' cunts! You wanted death, you got your death, how'd you like it?
How'd you like your eyes an' brains spread around, smeared on my boot?
Into the afterlife, with yer head kicked ter JAM?
Here's what you wanted,
where your MOUTH used to be!

Here's what you wanted,
where your DICK used to be!

CAI: Save it! Save it!

IESTYN: They say you shouldn't kick a man
when he's down, BOLLOCKS!
When he's just tried to kill you, it feels FUCKIN' MARVELLOUS! My joints an' muscle an' tongue still work, an' his are SMASHED. LOOK DOWN, BEHOLD MY WORK. ITS STRANGE BEAUTY. ITS – DISCLOSURE.

OWAIN: He stamps an' kicks till they are not just dead,
but human paste.

CAI: *(grabs IESTYN)* And now you stop.
Breathe in, the night air. Deep.
(IESTYN does so, subsides)
You save it, for the next one.

IESTYN: I will do that. *(Glares)* I will save it for the next one.

CAI: You follow me.
(They hike onwards)

OWAIN: We crawl up through the rocks in the moonlight,
lungs still on rapid fire. Same moon you see from

Wales. Except tonight it's pulsing. All the land around and beneath me is sendin' out a high pitched hum, an' Cai has this blistering bright blue flame all around him, but it must be me, still high on the epipen.
Hey, Iestyn, giss another song –

IESTYN: *(after reflection; to the tune of 'Nights in White Satin')*
'Nights in Prestatyn / Never reaching the end /
Never waste a sensation / Can I piss on your friend?'

OWAIN: 'Bunk-ups in Barmouth /
When you can't find the floor /
Just what my cock's in / I can't say any more' –

CAI: Quiet.

IESTYN: Up ahead!

CAI: Stand easy.

OWAIN: It's a man with an M16, ragged scarf, chest protector, Kevlar helmet: looks like an Iraqi soldier.
An insurgent?
An enemy's not likely to carry an M16;
but everything's mixed up now.

IESTYN: He's wearin' US Army desert camouflage
under his body armour.

We get close enough to see his eyes.
They're blue.

OWAIN: Am I hallucinatin'?

CAI: It's OK. This is my uncle.
Better man, than the father who left us.

IESTYN: *(aside)* Or is this the trap?

CAI: He don't speak: lost his tongue.
Now we call him Scratch. That's how he tells himself in his sign language: scratch on the ground, a scratch on the wall.

OWAIN: They clasp like old friends.
The old guy's mouth opens in a big grin.
A cheerful wound. Relieved to erupt.
Capable of spreadin' anywhere.
His fingers work, scrabblin' and gesturin' somethin' to Cai.
(Beat)
He hands a metal canister over to Cai.
An' Cai shakes his hand. I'm shakin', myself.
I punch my hands against my thighs,
tell myself to get a grip.

IESTYN: The uncle points to a cave. Cai motions us on, into it.
Oh fuck, this is it, one way or another.

OWAIN: We have to follow. We clamber up.
Cai stops at the mouth of the cave, says -

CAI: Tunnels. Fifteen years back, they dug down to the bottom of the mountain, built a network to avoid airstrikes and launch counterattacks.
But deserted when my uncle found it, an' set it up different, for him an' me. We call it:
The Anchorage. I want to show you: it's time.

OWAIN: Time for what?

CAI: But first: you present arms. *(Beat)* You have to roll up your sleeves. And hold out your fuckin' ARMS!

OWAIN: Cai has opened up the canister, revealing two hypodermics.
There's somethin' in his voice. Makes us do it.
Like we suddenly know, what we have to do, now.
An' it's a relief.

IESTYN: *(Complies, as if proposing/accepting a toast, to something highly honourable)* Hell an' back.

CAI: *(with significantly different emphasis)*
Hell an' BACK.

(IESTYN receives his shot, with a sharp intake of breath suggesting masochistic pleasure; CAI administers it with the formality and respect of pinning a medal on him.)

OWAIN: He is taking my wrist and turning it over,
stretching it out like a doctor or priest;
Then he looks up the forearm from wrist veins
to elbow joint;
Straightens my arm,
Takes a breath,
Sinks the needle in the flesh,
Plunges the syringe;
The blow that breaks the skin
Makes me gasp
Then comes the sting and soreness
Strangely sweet…
Like somethin's lifted off me,
out the back of my shoulders an' head.

(They all BREATHE: deeply).

OWAIN: We head on down.

(L/X, S/X: cave)

IESTYN: The stones of the path are slippy.

OWAIN: We duck our heads an' cramp our shoulders.

IESTYN: The air's not like you'd expect. It's warm; an' thin.

CAI: Down here: you find the secrets of the world.

IESTYN: And then the air opens out, cool and echoing like his voice.

OWAIN: We're in a cavern. A long high stone chamber.
Cai swings his torch beam round walls, that have been blackened by fires.

IESTYN: The light hits - animals, coiled, about to pounce?

OWAIN: I nearly scream out loud.
The torchlight hits the bodies of three
massive horses, entwined,
frozen frantic in the act of devouring each other.
One is clambering on the other's back but being pushed upwards, off-balance, its head at a sickening angle as the other bites out its throat.
The third, entangled, has its face thrust out between their legs, eyes blind with hopeless horror.
On their necks and flanks, the stone flesh hangs off them: like awful, ragged flowers.

IESTYN: They are bound round by serpents: wrapping them,
squeezing and twisting them to bursting point.
The knot of pain, tightening.
These serpents have – wings?

CAI: My uncle saw this statue: 'Duncan's Horses'.
A version of it stood in London Crystal Palace,
till it was destroyed, by fire.
People used to say, an untrained soldier couldn't
have made that, by himself. But there's another
version, a casting, in the Royal Veterinary College;
they only let you look at it, by prior appointment. It
inspired Uncle Scratch. To do some work of his
own. Like this. An' this -

OWAIN: Then Cai swings his light over the other side,
and up at another shape.
It's human but it has wings.
It wears a helmet but seems female; an angel,
but it's not serene.
It holds out two forearms,
brandishing stumps where there should be hands.
One of the wings hangs, wretched,
an' the bone sticks out broken.
Its nose has been sliced, an' opened out.
Eyes without eyelids, torn open to the world.
Its lipless jaw: showing yellow teeth and fangs,
transplanted from a huge dog.

CAI: Winged Victories are two a penny.
So we worked together, made this ourselves:
She's unique. She's the Spirit of Defeat.
What's left, after the frenzy: Our Lady of the Scorched Earth.

IESTYN: What the fuck? Is it a dummy - ?

CAI: It's an anatomical model that used to be in a surgeons' college. He added the wings and helmet,
I modified thc arms an' face.
But the main attraction is over here.

IESTYN: He shows us.
At the end of the cavern, a fucking four metre figure, looking back across at us, past the other statues, knowing they all lead up to him.

OWAIN: Christ almighty.

CAI: NO, something better than him.
Something unbeatable.
Lads: This is our God.
Santa Muerte.
This is Death.

OWAIN: This massive THING is crowned by a sort of tribal headdress that could be tangled worms.

The skin's flayed off his face,
he has deepset cunning eyes, an' his jaw is
hinged in an open laughscream.
His hands are upturned claws, accepting and
demanding all.

CAI: Four years, since my first trip out here,
we been workin' on these.
I come up here whenever I can: check on my uncle,
the conditions an' development of this.
Our work. We shoot up. An' we worship.
(*Gestures them to kneel*)
I thought it was time to share them. Selfish, not to.
They're the secrets of the world.
I thought: you might understand, an' appreciate.
Most importantly, I come back to
Rededicate myself.

OWAIN: You mean – to –

CAI: Death.

IESTYN: You spent years MAKIN' these fuckin' things?

CAI: We are manifestin': the unspeakable principles of
this world.
Fuck Redemption, 'greater good', crosses an'
crucifixions. That's to reassure frightened kids.

These show you the real deal.
Human bein's break. They're DESIGNED to.
They show the UTTER LOSS of CONTINUITY.
There are stories that go on, beyond them.
But they ain't told, or made, or understood: by anythin' that's human.

OWAIN: So when you've been goin' off radar –
you've been coming back to THIS PLACE?

CAI: It cuts through the shit.

IESTYN: (*Rises*) Jeezus, mun. I had you figured as turning over to AL-QAEDA.

CAI: They're still hung up on Sacrifice.
We're not that stupid.

IESTYN: You been buildin' an' keepin' these – ABORTIONS - in a cave in BAGHDAD?

CAI: Everyone will focus on the city, and the oil.
This is a 'Hide In Plain Sight' deal.
To stay undetected, you misdirect attention.
In Iraq, everyone else is lookin' for the second largest oil reserves on the planet.
Meanwhile, we've built a temple.
To the one creed, that crosses ALL the boundaries.

IESTYN: You gone PACIFIST?

CAI: Have I fuck.
Was I 'pacifist' back there, down the hill?
What I love about this stuff, is it tells you no lies.
Strips away the 'happy ever afters'. Makes you
see things, clean an' sharp. What the true soldier
knows. *(Beat)*
We serve Death. And we should serve Him,
in that knowledge.
A thorough dedication: to his principles;
an' his processes.
(Beat)
I dunno why you're so gobsmacked about this.
It's what you've allus gone after. Ecstasy an' *hwyl.*
That taste you found in your mouths tonight:
don't pretend you don't know it.
That made me think you were ready;
to come here, with me.

IESTYN: You have gone
Completely
An'
Clinically
Fuckin'
Mad Cow
Mental.
Why am I surprised?

Everything you've been through.
I've often STUCK UP for you, by tellin' others,
as how your bein' UNHINGED is what's given you
the crucial edge.
Your capacity to be even madder than those fuckers
we 'ave been fightin', Christ!
I should have seen this comin' years ago.

CAI: Look. What's the best word in this language?
The most thrilling? The most stirring?
It ain't 'money'. It ain't 'love'. It ain't 'cunt'.
It's COMBAT.
Thass the real gateway. Where you find the true measure of a man: the place an' time he welcomes Death. When he turns his pain into pride. We have to let our misery shape us, 'cos it's irresistible; but we don't let it limit us. We find a purpose, which makes us bigger than our pain. Soldiers work with suffering: it's their material, like a carpenter works with wood. We make sculptures out of pain, an' we learn how to do it with craft and skill. We take other people's bodies to where they have to feel and show their amazement: in that moment, of COMBAT. When your every hair and nerve are screamingly alive, because someone is trying to blow them apart forever; where the only thing that can save you is the power of your will, to be stronger than theirs, in action.
COMBAT.
Only source of honour. Doorway to Death.

IESTYN: Yer OFF YER HEAD. Everythin' changes, if you just switch the first letter of that word. Make it 'WOMBAT'. *(Beat)*
'Hand to hand wombat'. *(Beat)*
'Wombat fatigues'. *(Beat)*
S'not the same, is it?

OWAIN: I know how it might sound strange…
(It's a stoned-sincere revelation)
But I actually think some kinda CRAZY PINOCCHIO ought to be in there amongst 'em. No, really, I do. A WOOD SUPREMACIST, threatenin' ter STOP people bein' real live boys – *(CAI takes this as sarcasm)*

CAI: You two. I don't know why I bothered t'save your ARSES back there. Oh sure, you can sneer at anything if you want to. Skip the body armour, thanks, we've got Irony.
No need to engage, no need for courage, no need for LIFE. No respect for Death.

IESTYN: WHO SAYS YOU CAN SAY, I GOT NO NEED FOR MY LIFE? JUST BECAUSE YOU'RE OUTSIDE OF IT, NOT INSIDE IT LIKE ME.

OWAIN: *(Rises: aside)* My body and my mind are just this one big frenzied burning itch an' *(out loud)*

I just don’t know what’s real anymore.

CAI: Well, maybe YOU ain’t real. Maybe I am just makin’ you up. In a dream; or a fuckin’ nightmare, more like.

IESTYN: You are one crazed cunt. Jesus, Owain, we should have taken him out when we had a chance.

CAI: What d’you mean: ‘taken me out’?

OWAIN: Cai: we were asked to keep you under close surveillance. The Boss thought you might have gone native, turned Al-Qaeda. But now we can tell him, he was wrong, you’re still loyal –

IESTYN: LOYAL? LOYAL TO WHAT? He ain’t SANE.
(Beat)

CAI: YOU. Were gonna TAKE ME OUT???
Iestyn, the things we’ve done an’ seen together.
An’ you an’ Scratch, here, you patrolled the Falls Road side by side, watchin’ each others’ backs.

IESTYN: An’ now you’re two crazy death-worshippers.
You stay the fuck away from me, you bleedin’ bomb-happy GOTHS.
(Beat)

CAI: Thass funny you say that: cos the Roman Empire was brought down by the Goths.
They were the soldiers it trained and paid.
Then they wised up.
They took the fuckin' game apart.
(Beat)
I just saved your lives.
Then I brought you here because I figured we could finally trust each other. More fool me.

OWAIN: We had orders, to – sound you out.
We had clearance to –
(deliberately throws away the words)
use force if we 'ad to –

CAI: You were preparin' to kill me.
Even after I saved your lives,
you were ready to kill me, on an order from someone who's never set foot in this place.
Who ignores any details about a situation, that don't fit with the orders they get.
(Becomes tearful: in a strangely boyish profound disappointment)
Oh, you fuckers.
I thought we were mates.
I thought we 'ad a bond.
I shoulda known.
Same thing, as ever.

OWAIN: The old man, Scratch: falls to his knees, in prayer.
Starts this high-pitched keening.

CAI: *(Collects himself, with dangerous speed and intentness)*
So what exactly were you scared I'd do?
What are you scared I'll do now?
Bet you I can come up with somethin' worse
than you can ever imagine.
I'm a good soldier.
A very good soldier, boys.
I'm throwin' it down.
You pickin' it up?
Are you pickin' it up?

IESTYN: Cai – look – we was just followin' orders.

CAI: Just followin' orders?
Right.
(His throat clears)
I see now.
Of course.
I understand you.
C'mere.
Cwtch.

(CAI extends his arms in a disarming embrace. After a hesitation of trying to fathom him, IESTYN laughs, relaxes, walks into the embrace. CAI starts to sing. Recognizing the tune, the others give a brief grunt or snort of relief.)

Os treisiodd y gelyn fy ngwlad tan ei droed,

Mae hen iaith y Cymry mor fyw ag erioed,

Ni luddiwyd yr awen gan erchyll law brad,

(CAI clasps IESTYN's head, swings him round [downstage], drives his thumbs into his eyes. IESTYN gasps, screams as appallingly as is humanly possible.)

Na thelyn berseiniol fy ngwlad.

(CAI sings louder through his teeth and effort, holding IESTYN in an iron grip which contains the struggling, singing louder over the screaming, pushing IESTYN to his knees, moving his hands to a throttling grip: IESTYN now sobs and chokes)

Gwlad, gwlad, pleidiol wyf i'm gwlad.
Tra môr yn fur i'r bur hoff bau,
O bydded i'r hen iaith barhau.

(Song concluded, he releases IESTYN, whose body slumps to the ground)

OWAIN: The old man has stopped his wailing.
Just kneels there, like he's petrified…

CAI: *(As if he sees the body for the first time)*
Oh fuckin' hell. I've done it AGAIN.
(CAI starts to shake. OWAIN approaches with calming noises, getting closer)

OWAIN: Breathe deep, Cai...

CAI: It's Death, Owain.
It bloody came, and it bloody will again.
Nothing wants me, only Death.

OWAIN: Cai. I know: Death ain't ready for you yet.

CAI: 'Ow do you know, mun? I know 'im better than you.
Death's my father, Owain. I ain't got no other father.
I ain't ever gonna be a father. I can't be part o' any chain
that stretches from the past into the future.
All I find is - severance. All I know is severance. I sever

things. Even when I don't want to.

So I try to learn to love it. Do it for a living. Fuck,

I don't know anything else.

OWAIN: Hey, c'mon – we'll get you out of here,

take you back to Wales –

CAI: What can Wales offer me, 'cept the smell of sheep shit?

Look at me shakin', Owain, like an old *cymro.*

You know, the way they see you out walkin' on a

hill, or down a track, an' they tell you 'THIS IS MY

PRIVATE LAND, GET OFF MY PRIVATE LAND',

(he speaks these words of savagely insistent determinism with the performance of a Parkinsons quiver)

t'show they're sure about how 'everythin'-will-be',

like they're callin' the faithful to prayer. All that

bitterness an' resentment, congealed. Calcified.

Into knots of bone. An' all those clumpy fists just

shake themselves against the world; shake in the

knowledge o' their OWN IMPOTENCE – *(Beat)*

Thass Wales, Owain. A valley of knotted bone.

OWAIN: No. It don't have to be like that, Cai.

Look: you gotta trust me.

CAI: Whenever I trust people, they go wrong.

An' Death steps in. I try to accept it, get used to it,

even expect it. 'Cos it's what we all come to.

OWAIN: Yeah, but Iestyn was followin' orders.

Cai: I have stopped followin' orders. I promise you.

(Beat)

Now: do you promise me? To stop followin' orders?

From the Brits? An' from the old quiverin' *cymry*?

(Beat)

An' even yer uncle? Ain't true nothin' wants you.

I want you. Deal with it.

CAI: What?

OWAIN: It ain't true, that every man wants to come to death.

If you touch a man right, he comes to life.

Promise me to stop followin' orders?

CAI: Prove it.

OWAIN: What?

CAI: Touch me.

(Hesitation is overcome. They embrace, briefly.)

I promise you.

(An effect of time: desert wind)

OWAIN: *(isolated in single spot: aside to audience)*

It's true. He'd got inside my veins.

He deserves better than this place. We ALL do.

We leave the cave. I send word back that Iestyn had been killed by an insurgent. I'm not too proud of that. Uncle Scratch doesn't stop us, or even look at Cai. He just stands lookin' at the figures they'd made. Like he was gettin' a new idea, for another. He can look after himself. He knows the terrain. Then me an' Cai disappear. Through Syria and Istanbul. Tangiers. Discoverin' new ways: to use lips, an' eyelids: an' everything.

Every time he holds me, I know he could snap.

And snap me.

Each embrace: could be a strangulation.

I tell him: I'm there for him.

And he's made me a promise.

Sometimes, he says, us two Goths should head

back to Rome. Show 'em what we've learnt.

Sometimes I remind him, we ain't seen Ruthin yet.

I know what they call me.

I know what I am.

'Bloody nympho'.

'OCD sex addict'.

An' I bloody love it.

I need him. Not once but several times a day.

I don't wanna be cured. I ain't pork. Not yet.

I've watched one man turn another into meat;

an' I've done it myself.

Made someone into meat. Before he could do it to me.

Cai's my cure. He's my poison.

I wanna be poisoned. Thoroughly.

We go inside each other.

So I'm the pulse, inside his body.

Then he's the pulse, inside o' mine.

An' that's what I wanna take to my grave.

An' beyond it, if I can.

'Cause there's nothing better, that I've found.

So why shouldn't I?

You jealous?

Well, *I* ain't gonna stop *you.*

I ain't stoppin' you

I ain't stoppin' myself

I ain't stoppin' him

I ain't stoppin'

Sure: sometimes I think:

He'll be the death of me.

I know what I am.

I seen worse ways to die.

*   *   *

(Fade to black. Band Pres Llareggub's 'Cwm Rhondda', feat. Lisa Jên, from 0:50 in, till end, for Curtain Call. Fucking Loud.)

Going down: *eros, thanatos*, and the politically transformative potential of queer desire in David Ian Rabey's *Land of My Fathers* and *Last Ditch*

by *Lara Maleen Kipp*

Readers will forgive me the titular innuendo of this essay – of course it is there deliberately, but not facetiously. In its spatial meaning, it alludes to the notion of *katabasis*, the mythical journey into, and ultimately through death, a movement of dissolution, discovery, and ultimately transformation. In its sexual meaning, it offers a focus on desire, on deliberately non-reproductive pleasure, which recalls resistance to those socially dominant constructions of meaningful life, love, and death, which centre on a futurity contingent on heteronormative reproduction.

As such, this essay considers manifestations of *eros* (drive to life and pleasure) and *thanatos* (drive to death and destruction) in David Ian Rabey's plays *Land of My Fathers* (2018) and *Last Ditch (Anrhefn yng Nghymru)* (2023) as transformative forces. In particular, the plays employ the mythological and alchemical principle of *katabasis*, which I here propose acts in conjunction, though not always harmony, with *eros* and *thanatos*. I compare the relationships of Owain and Cai in the former play, and various constellations of characters in the latter. Both plays offer inquiries into the human search for meaning and connection, and in both cases, it is queer desire that offers not solutions, but at least a way forward. These plays interrogate notions of nationhood, masculinity, and their entanglement, while proposing a transformative queer ethics rooted in descent, disruption, and rebirth.

Before delving into the plays, I must outline some key concepts and their definitions. *Eros* here refers not only to a will to live, but moreover a drive to pleasure and connection, transcendent of rationality. *Thanatos* on the other hand, is not merely a destructive or nihilistic drive. On the contrary, it is much more aligned with the figure of Death as it appears in tarot: in every ending, there is a beginning, and so the drive to destruction is also one of creation. It 'challenges everything that exists [but] it is also a will to begin from zero' (Dean, 2008: 131), and as such, *eros* and *thanatos* are not diametrically opposed, but entwined. I define queer here in line with Campbell and Farrier, who in turn reference Halperin, as something or someone being at odds with the dominant system and hierarchy (2016), namely phallogocentric, heteronormative Western capitalist patriarchy. I define ethics in line with Davé, as a reflective, emergent process interrogating moral principles in a 'creative, disruptive response to the drive to normalization' (2010: 374). Within this definition, the alignment of queer and ethics already emerges; queer ethics, for my purposes here, is thus a process that is consciously at odds with dominant systems and narratives insofar as it exposes their constructed nature by way of pluralistic interrogation. Davé's emphasis on creativity and disruption seems particularly apt, not just for the theatrical context of this essay, but for fundamental ideas that Rabey's playwriting contends with, as will emerge over the course of this essay.

Having provided readers with some key definitions, I want to turn to discussing each play in turn, beginning with *Land of My Fathers*. On the surface, the play offers an exploration of nationhood, masculinity, and (post)colonialism in the story of British agents posing as private military contractors in Afghanistan and Iraq, seeking to determine if one or more of their colleagues has "gone native". On a deeper level, it expands into considerations of national and cultural identity with regards to Welsh identity in Britain, and the entanglement of neoliberal capitalism and imperialist ideology.

In the pre-script, that is, prior to the play text proper, Rabey offers several extracts from diverse sources. Supposedly, these set the mood and orient a reader of the play, as well as any director and company engaging with the material; to audiences, these snippets likely remain invisible. I want to highlight a few here that support my thesis of the play text as one that proposes queer desire inclusive of a transformative death drive (cf. Dean, 2008). Rabey quotes Gurney who proposes that 'the love of comrades sweetens all' (this volume: 154), to me an allusion to the homosexual desire that emerges as a surprising (ir)resolution at the end of the play. Consider this alongside O'Brien's lines: 'To dance freestyle; /For your partner, Death/ [...] Through a dark stone hall' (*ibid*: 155). Here, the *jouissance* of unstructured movement, is oriented towards *thanatos*, and the image of the 'dark stone hall' brings to mind a *chthonic* journey in the vein of Greek and Roman mythology. Before the play itself begins therefore, the pre-script thus offers thematic impulses that introduce notions of both *eros* and *thanatos*, as well as queer desire.

Equally, the entanglement of the two drives arises in the opening monologue by Owain as he describes the erotically charged transformation triggered by the handling of a gun:

> The hand will lead, the spine will stretch, the feet will spread; the buttocks will tighten, the head will tilt, the brows will darken with slyness an' power. [...] I feel the halo of the crosswires, the Benediction of the Seeping Red. We drink it in with our father's spunk. (this volume: 159-60)

While this speech might be read in terms of male bravado and deliberate crassness, alluding as it does to the opening motif of a James Bond film, designed to establish dominance beyond the behavioural norms of civilian life, I would propose that the opening text offers the first inklings of queer desire, by way of its sensual depiction of the male body. Its lingering on male physique and explicit references to buttocks and ejaculate invite queer readings.

The scene in the pub which follows shortly thereafter, then introduces the notion of *katabasis,* with explicit references to the 'overworld' and 'underworld' (*ibid.*: 167). More importantly, it establishes Cai's desire to 'be the hero of two worlds' (*ibid.*), a desire he identifies as the 'Welsh dream' (*ibid.*). This he sets out in contrast to the obvious, loud American Dream of Manifest Destiny one the one hand, and insipid English repression on the other. Additionally, this exchange includes a reference to the *Mabinogion*, in which *annwn*, the underworld (or otherworld), plays a significant role, not least for the mythological hero Pwyll (Roberts, 2005: 371-372).

The introduction of Welsh mythology as something which offers a distinct and alternative narrative, one which operates on a both/and principle (cf. Kipp, 2020), establishes the possible co-existence and intermingling of seemingly opposing forces: *eros* and *thanatos*, or as Iestyn puts it, the 'WHIFF of combined attraction AND antagonism' (this volume: 186). The play deliberately engages the colonial trope of (White, Western, male) heroes journeying into the (corrupting, foreign, less-than, in need of civilising) Middle East. This is crucially motivated by the fear of the powers-that-be – exemplified by the un-named, de-individuated, cog-in-the-system Chief – that one of their own might have "gone native", *ergo* abandoned his duty, and station, by way of abandoning the ideal of White, British, straight, cis, hetero man. Rabey satirises this trope, deconstructing it over the course of the play. He achieves this not only by way of Iestyn's exaggerated description of Iraq as 'a cathedral of debris, irrigated by infectious sewage [...], a sort of maddening bouncy-castle-labyrinth' (this volume: 189), but by the fact that this echoes Owain's disdainful account of his valley town home as 'Cwm Puke' (*ibid.*: 174). Evidently, the issue is not the place, but within the people, their attitudes, and limited imaginations for how else to live their lives beyond neoliberal capitalist structures.

Importantly, Rabey does not offer up a romanticised vision of Welsh nationalism as counterpoint, but skewers any impulse towards such simplistic substitution by way of Nigel Jenkins's parody version of the Welsh national anthem (*ibid.*: 195) and later Russ Gomer/David Garland Jones's revised lyrics for Bachman-Turner Overdrive's 'You Ain't Seen Nothing Yet' (*ibid.*: 207). Additionally, Iestyn's rant about Iraq offers imagery that foreshadows the later movement of physical and psychic descent. This is achieved by references to volcanos and a labyrinth – the former famously acting as gates to the underworld in Greek mythology, and the latter figuring as a dangerous space of transformation. In both cases, there be monsters, not least 'The Minotaur of Anticipation. Squattin' in the Maze of Logic' (*ibid.*: 203).

The final passage before Part 2 offers equally resonant lines which conjure the notion of *katabasis* before the characters actually begin their physical descent into the cave system in the hills. Notably, Iestyn declares the events to come 'the ultimate test' (*ibid.*: 212), conjuring the transformative hero's journey of various myths; though in his understanding of the test to come, he anticipates betrayal by

Cai in a much more pedestrian manner than is to follow. The impending journey into the underworld is also metaphorically invoked by Owain and Cai, who conceive their impending conflict in terms of 'Bringin' the hell' and 'Spreadin' it around, chasin' it back, to where it needs to go' (*ibid.*: 213). At this point, *thanatos* goes into overdrive, exemplified in Cai's declaration: 'We make friends with Death. We extend it to those we meet. […] We work with it, to speed up the process. The deathspeed. That's us' (*ibid.*: 213). Nonetheless, this death drive is also tinged with *eros* in the sensorily charged invitation to '[b]athe in [death], taste it, embrace it, kiss it, swallow it, […] become it' (*ibid.*: 214)., a desire for self-annihilation by way of ecstatic union with a radically different other. This layering of the two drives in especially pronounced in Cai, and comes to the fore again in the ambush scene: his invocation of the Egyptian notion of Ka (*ibid.*: 217-8) alludes to life after death, and his description of the slow motion experience of mortal combat is in no uncertain terms linked to *eros* when he explains to the audience to 'treat every moment like it is great sex' (*ibid.*: 218). The aftermath of the battle not only merges both drives, too, but also offers the first more explicit homoerotic moment when Owain muses that one of their local guides is looking 'strangely attractive. Wall-eyed an' hairy an' yet – seductive' (*ibid.*: 224). After the extremely violent encounter at the shepherd's hut, Cai convinces the others to follow him into the hills where they meet his uncle and the *katabasis* proper begins.

The journey into the cave system begins with accepting an altered state of consciousness in the form of an unknown drug (*ibid.*: 230) that will take the characters to '[h]ell an' BACK' (*ibid.*: 230-1). I want readers to pay close attention to Owain's sexually charged language as he consents to his shot, administered by Cai:

> Then he *looks up the forearm from wrist veins to elbow joint*;
>
> Straightens my arm,
>
> Takes a breath,
>
> *Sinks* the needle in the flesh,
>
> *Plunges* the syringe;
>
> The blow that breaks the skin
>
> *Makes me gasp*
>
> Then comes the *sting and soreness*
>
> *Strangely sweet…*
>
> *Like somethin's lifted off me, out the back of my shoulders an' head.*
>
> (*ibid.*: 231; my emphasis)

First, the visual caress of exposed skin, then the double penetrative movement of the needle and syringe, the breathless response, followed by somewhat masochistic pleasure that dissolves into ecstasy. Then follows the journey downward, to the 'secrets of the world' (*ibid.*: 232). Understanding this as *katabasis* is not speculation, but confirmed as such by the author, who in his Foreword to this play identifies this as a principle he embraced, denoting Rudkin's *The Sons of Light* as an influence, with conscious parallels in his own play.

Following the murder of Iestyn – which readers might interpret as a violent divestment from romanticised notions of a heteronormative, male-coded Welsh nationalism, given that it occurs alongside the national anthem – queer desire comes to the fore as a force that is able to disentangle *eros* and *thanatos*:

CAI:	It's Death, Owain. [...] Nothing wants me, only Death. [...]
OWAIN:	[...] Ain't true nothin' wants you.
	I want you.
	Deal with it.
CAI:	What?
OWAIN:	It ain't true, that every man wants to come to death.
	If you touch a man right, he comes to life.
	Promise me to stop followin' orders?
CAI:	Prove it.
OWAIN:	What?
CAI:	Touch me.
	(Hesitation is overcome. They embrace, briefly.)
	I promise you.
	(*ibid.*: 246-7)

In this expression of queer desire, not only is the death drive transmuted into a drive to pleasurable life, but the trope of the hero's journey is also subverted. Owain and Cai do not emerge from the caves to reintegrate into the existing systems and hierarchies. Neither are *eros* and *thanatos* completely separated, after all, they are not binary opposites *per se*:

OWAIN: [...] He deserves better than this place. We ALL do.
We leave the cave. [...]
Then me an' Cai disappear. [...]
Discoverin' new ways: to use lips, an' eyelids:
an' everything.
Every time he holds me, I know he could snap.
And snap me. Each embrace: could be a strangulation. [...]
I need him. Not once but several times a day. [...]
We go inside each other.
So I'm the pulse, inside his body.
Then he's the pulse, inside o' mine.
An' that's what I wanna take to my grave.
An' beyond it, if I can. [...]
Sure: sometimes I think:
He'll be the death of me.
I know what I am.
I seen worse ways to die.
(*ibid.*: 247-9)

Owain's final monologue thus offers the audience a sensuous alternative to the limitations of heteronormative necropolitics. Instead, his relationship with Cai becomes a radical alternative, a queer ethics of deeply embodied equality that needs continuous attending and reinvestment. Owain and Cai's relationship transforms *eros* and *thanatos* into creative – though crucially not productive! – existence, allowing them to find liberation in the flesh of each other.

Last Ditch (Anhrefn yng Nghymru) (2020) offers some similar considerations, though narratively, the connection to *katabasis* is less immediately apparent. The title page identifies the play as a 'spiritual-political extravaganza', which thus clearly states its main concerns: matters of the soul, and matters of power distribution. The play's summary, as offered by the dramatist in an interview (Rabey 2023: 38), includes the play's heroes being on a mission to 'counter a slide into cosmic suicide' – countering *thanatos* – and seeking to 'effect a worldwide cultural and spiritual transformation' (*ibid.*). *Katabatic* resonances chime through in Rabey's identification of the play as a 'struggle for the terms of existence' (*ibid.*) and 'wild laughter in the face of death' (*ibid.*) – to confront death, and move through and beyond it. Additionally, the play's sections are named after the four alchemical stages, nigredo, albedo, citrinitas, and rubedo. The first is associated with blackening and decomposition and, in Jungian psychology, with plunging into the dark night of the soul for the purpose of transformation (Miller, 2004: 114). Notably, Miller, referencing Schwartz-Salant, describes this in decidedly death-associated terms, summarising nigredo as 'state of disorganization and putrefaction that breaks and transforms things' (*ibid.*). This aligns with Dean's interpretation of Lacan, for whom *thanatos* holds both creative and destructive potential (2008: 130) – and so does *eros*. Both drives also contain movements towards dissolution of self (cf. Gritzner, 2010: 5-7).

The prologue of *Last Ditch* also alludes to *katabatic* movements, conjuring 'a rise AND a fall' (this volume: 17) and alluding to the underworld river Styx (*ibid.*: 17), and the Nietzschean abyss of the soul looking back at the subject trying to confront its unknown depths (*ibid.*: 18). Further, *thanatos* haunts the prologue with its mentions of depth, damage, and breaking (*ibid.*: 18), shadows and spirits (*ibid.*: 20), and *katabatic* transformation presents itself in the image of shedding skins (ibid.: 19).

The descending movement that begins the journey of *katabasis* is present in several forms, more or less explicit: Tanwen's first line is, 'this is the beginning of the end' (*ibid.*: 23); Dyfrig's use of the same line is followed almost immediately by his declaration of love for Gwenllian (*ibid.*: 27), introducing an erotic impulse alongside the acknowledgement of impending doom. More explicitly, Tanwen reaches her dark night of the soul in the riot police's interrogation chamber (*ibid.*: 33), which is immediately juxtaposed with the 'sexual electricity' between Aisling and Ronan (*ibid.*: 34), and thereafter returns to Tanwen, '*broken in many ways'* (*ibid.*: 36). Here, Rabey sets up *eros* and *thanatos* side-by-side, and their intermingling offers the first stage of descent, disintegration, and darkness, which is necessary before transformation can occur.

The next section introduces the non-human characters, including manifestations of chaos, Annie, who I propose also personifies *eros*; the spirit of fear and destruction, personifying *thanatos*, M; the angel and chronicler of death, Boneblack; and the ineffable, elusive Rubato, later introduced by Annie as 'The Genius of Time' (*ibid.*: 82). To characterise this figure, the playwright helpfully pointed me to the word's definition in terms of musical tempo: 'the freedom or flexibility to choose your own tempo for a part or a phrase' (in private email exchange). Given the origins of the notion of genius as an attendant spirit, much like muses, I am therefore tempted to describe Rubato as the manifestation of choice and free will. Combined with the closeness of his name with final alchemical stage, *rubedo*, which in Jungian terms refers to the emergence of a unified psyche, a new self with integrated conscious and unconscious, and irreversible transmutation (Mathers, 2014: 251), readers might thus circumscribe their understanding of this character. He, when visiting the humans, frames transformation in terms that I argue are erotically charged: 'Transformation will require you to SWEAT / And to PANT, till your snatched breath starts to turn you into someone else entirely' (*ibid.*: 89). He then instructs them to dig ('Cloddia', *ibid.*), once again introducing a (metaphorical) downward, inward, movement. It is also important to note that Rubato's harsh address to the Mayflies echoes José Esteban Muñoz's assertion that hope is work and disappointment will happen, but this does not cancel all hope, not does it diminish the necessity for working to change things (Chambers-Letson et al., 2019: x). This necessity to work, in spite of everything, to me invokes a queer ethics that rejects the *status quo* and instead demands to imagine other ways of being (cf. Wachowski in Chambers-Letson et al., 2019: xiii). Crucially, Rabey's play frames this not as a disengagement or dismissal of what is, and/or a naïve escape into dreaming of a "better" future, but rather the necessary creative, disruptive labour of contending with, and working to dismantle, the dominant structures of heteronormative, patriarchal capitalism. Annie, the angel of anarchy and independence undergoes her own *katabasis*, after all she steps '*over into Downstairs*' (this volume: 77), on a journey of self-transformation, even as she does not set out with that specific goal. Her queer-coding becomes apparent when she introduces herself to Tanwen as, among other things, 'Polly Amorous' (*ibid.*: 80), flirting with both Tanwen and an audience member (*ibid.*). As such, *eros* emerges as a queer transformative impulse, albeit one that cannot be controlled, and the chaos is both thrilling and devastating (*ibid.*: 80). I must note here that the playwright clarified in our email exchange that he wrote the character as bisexual, explicitly and consciously expanding the spectrum of attractions represented in this play. Before I return to the movement of Annie's *katabasis*, and the role queer desire ultimately plays in it, I want to turn to two further moments: Catrin and Aisling, and The Lynx's invocation and animation of statues, respectively.

Following Rubato's visit, Catrin and Aisling fall in love (*ibid.*: 91), their lesbian relationship pulling the latter out of the pit of despair she finds herself in after her former lover's[1] suicide and her own terminal diagnosis. Following Tanwen's magical healing intervention (*ibid.*: 93), itself 'strangely intimate' (*ibid.*), Aisling appears 'ecstatic' (*ibid.*: 96). *Eros,* specifically by way of queer desire, has moved her outside of herself, transformed her beyond her previous state of being. It is this 'intoxicated, euphoric' (*ibid.*: 137) state of queer desire that allows the two women to 'dream [themselves] into new shapes' (*ibid.*: 139), and to begin the ascent of the final leg of the *katabatic* journey: to soar and to rebuild (*ibid.*).

The Lynx, identified by Annie as a being who 'can dissolve the boundaries between the living and the dead' (*ibid.*: 102) and by himself as 'Guardian doorman at the portal of the possible' (*ibid.*: 104), invokes *thanatos* in his

---

[1] Ronan, making Aisling bi- or pansexual, too.

dismissal of self-preservation instincts (*ibid.*) before he sends out the call to animate statues and ceramics the world over (*ibid.*: 106-7). The destructive and (re)generative, creative consequences of this upheaval are explicitly addressed: 'Things WILL rumble apart: an' recombine / [...] Spreadin' the life around' (*ibid.*: 107) in a cataclysm that is nonetheless explicitly sexual, and *eros*-driven. Statues 'FUCK. Loudly and passionately' (*ibid.*: 109), *eros* and *thanatos* flow together, violently, in a 'union of opposites' (*ibid.*). A statue of Baphomet declares 'Let's get the Sex Magic Party STARTED!' (*ibid.* 110), while the fascist athletes depicted in the Stadio dei Marmi '[let] their innate camp tendencies flourish' (*ibid.:* 111), seducing members of a homophobic rally into 'raging queerness' (*ibid.*: 112) and they 'proceed to get down, deep into the groove' (*ibid.*), conjuring this chapter's titular innuendo and downward movement.

The *katabatic* imagery continues: 'Her proudly naked sister sends a pulse: down into the ocean bed. Beneath the crustacean bed, something is unmooring, and unfolding, with a seismic force...' (*ibid.*: 112). This pulse 'digs deeper' (*ibid.*: 113) and the resulting emergence of queer transformative impulses overcomes the *thanatotic* inertia of established necropolitical systems. This triggers an equally erotic dissolution of boundaries the world over, as statues 'meld, embrace and flow into and out of each other' (*ibid.*: 114), so humans are moved to tears and urgent sexual congress (*ibid.*) in which they may lose their established self and emerge with another. The transformative potential of queer desire, driven by both *eros* and *thanatos,* potentially destructive 'anger, and [possibly generative] longing' (*ibid.*: 116), is thus exemplified in the Lynx's call to action.

Before I attempt to bring both plays together in the conclusion, I want to highlight Annie's last *katabatic* movement. Returning from the human world, she addresses Boneblack:

> Just for now: look at that lovely friction.
>
> Trans-mission. Con-fusion.
>
> Look at those two, drawing deep on each others' breath,
>
> Them, tearin' open their shirts an' twiddlin' each others' sexberries:
>
> Look at them, amusin' their bouches with stiffy cocky puddin';
>
> Look at her, ecstatic at havin' her downward duct licked an' sucked.
>
> Boneblack: *I envy them.* (*ibid*: 122: my emphasis)

The confluence of energies and people eradicate previously seemingly stable boundaries, cutting across (trans) and bringing together (con), in explicitly sexual, but decidedly not reproductive terms. Here, Rabey's play taps into a sense of queer utopian futurity that to me aligns with Muñoz rethinking of Edelmann

(2004). Unlike Edelmann's purely *thanatotic* pessimism, Muñoz offers a conception of queer futurity, in which queerness is 'based on an economy of desire and desiring' (2019: 26), and futurity escapes the restrictions of 'reproductive majoritarian heterosexuality' (*ibid.*: 22); instead, queer futurity offers a 'new temporality [...] where the future is a site of infinite and immutable potentiality' (*ibid.*: 127). This fragile, hopeful potentiality, Annie envies, resulting in her provocative suggestion to Boneblack to 'try out some things' (this volume: 125). This also informs her approach to M, whom she draws into a 'long, slow, passionate kiss' (*ibid.*: 134). Rabey identified Annie's proposition in our correspondence as inviting M into 'a profoundly hopeful and fearless alchemical union of opposites'. While M is initially resistant, he ultimately consents and they leave together, *eros* and *thanatos* startlingly united (*ibid*: 135). Here, again, I see resonant interfaces with Muñoz. As Chambers-Letson et al. write in their foreword, Muñoz

> warned us against disappearing wholly into futurity, since "one cannot afford" to simply "turn away from the present." The present demands our ethical consideration and the task at hand is [...] to manoeuvre [*sic*] from the present's vantage point at the crossroads of life that is lived *after* catastrophe (as may be the case with queer, black, and brown life) and simultaneously *before* it. (2019: xiv; original emphases)

In employing the trope of *katabasis*, but refusing the typical reintegration of the hero into society upon their return, Rabey's playwriting invites readers (and even more so viewers of theatrical productions) to imagine beyond: beyond rigid binaries of life and death and especially what makes a life worth living; beyond how the world is "here and now" to how it might be. These invitations to imagine "beyond" are entangled with apparitions of queer desire in these plays: it is queer desire's fundamentally ethical impulse to disrupt and interrogate dominant systems, hierarchies, and drives to maintain reproductive heteronormativity, and propose alternative ways of thinking and being in the world (cf. Davé, 2010: 374) that Rabey's protagonists move towards. I once more turn to Muñoz, as his introduction to *Cruising Utopia* summarises beautifully how I understand the politically transformative potential of queer desire in Rabey's two plays:

> Queerness is a structuring and educated mode of desiring that allows us to see and feel beyond the quagmire of the present. [...] We must strive [...] we must dream and enact new and better pleasures, other ways of being in the world, and ultimately new worlds. (2019: 1)

To see and feel beyond the present, to dream and enact new and better pleasures, new ways of being and new worlds: what better place to begin this imagining in, than the theatre?

REFERENCES:

Cambell, A. and Farrier, S. (2016) 'Introduction' in Cambell, A. and Farrier, S. (eds.) *Queer Dramaturgies*, Basingstoke: Palgrave Macmillan, pp. 1-26

Davé, N. N. (2010) 'Between Queer Ethics and Sexual Morality' in Lambek, M. (ed.) *Ordinary Ethics*, New York: Fordham University Press, pp. 368-375

Dean, T. (2008) 'An Impossible Embrace: Queerness, Futurity, and the Death Drive' in Bono, J.J. (ed.) *A Time for the Humanities*, New York: Fordham University Press, pp. 122-140

Edelmann, L. (2004) *No Future: Queer Theory and the Death Drive*, Durham, NC: Duke University Press

Gritzner, K. (2010) 'Introduction' in Gritzner, K. (ed.) *Eroticism and Death in Theatre and Performance*, Hatfield: University of Hertfordshire Press, pp. 1-10

Kipp, L.M. (2020) *The Scenography of Howard Barker*, London and New York: Routledge

Mathers, Dale (2014) *Alchemy and Psychotherapy: Post-Jungian Perspectives*, New York: Routledge

Miller, J. C. (2004) *The Transcendent Function: Jung's Model of Psychological Growth through Dialogue with the Unconscious*, New York: State University of New York Press

Muñoz, J. E. (2019) *Cruising Utopia: The Then and There of Queer Futurity (The 10th Anniversary Edition)*, New York: New York University Press

Rabey, David Ian (2023) '*Last Ditch: An Interview with David Ian Rabey*' in The EGO magazine, no. 107 (Sept/Medi 2023), pp. 38-40. Bow Street, Ceredigion: Aberystwyth Ego Limited.

Roberts, B. F. (2005) 'Annwn' in Jones, L. (ed.) *Encyclopedia of Religion*, Gale eBooks, pp. 371-372

‘Parasitic Scenographics’: a critical reflection on the digital scenography design for David Ian Rabey’s *Land of My Fathers* and *Last Ditch* by *Piotr Woycicki*

This chapter is accompanied by a website that contains colour images and animations of the concepts discussed. References to animations are in the footnotes. Please visit the website as you read for further references. Website link: https://parasiticscenographics.myportfolio.com/

Figures marked * are available on the website only.

This chapter examines the role of the digital scenography I designed for the productions of David Ian Rabey’s *Land of My Fathers* (2018) and *Last Ditch* (2023). Both productions were staged at the Castle Theatre in Aberystwyth and directed by David Ian Rabey, with the latter being co-directed by Oliver Turner. For this reflection, I am interested in how digital scenography can function as a critical discourse on the socio-political themes espoused in the piece. I will investigate this by considering Elfriede Jelinek’s concept of the ‘secondary play’, or ‘parasitic play’ (in Juers-Munby 2013: 211) as Karen Juers-Munby conceptualised it. I apply this concept to the dramaturgical functions of digital scenography and consider what I will call ‘parasitic scenographics’. The chapter thus explores how the digital scenography designed for these two pieces positions itself in a ‘parasitic’ relationship to their dramatic material, a particular form of ‘visual dramaturgy’ (Lehmann, 2006). It explores how it visually juxtaposes ideas from the plays, effectuating instances of iconoclasm, parody, and satire. It also considers how it re-contextualises scenarios, furthers critical political commentaries, and establishes a network of correspondences and intertextualities that enmesh the two performances. I also draw upon Rosi Braidotti’s concept of ‘assemblages’ (Braidotti, 2018: 2-3) to analyse the multi-layered nature of the digital scenographic designs in the two productions and their ‘intermedial’ (Chapple and Kattenbelt, 2006) dramaturgy.

Before analysing my two case studies, I first outline the theoretical contexts that inform my examination of digital scenography in these productions. Given that both were ‘practice-as-research’ projects (Nelson, 2022), this section introduces key theoretical foundations and provide a methodological rationale for analysing the scenography’s critical function. It is also worth noting that I frequently engage with critical theoretical concepts throughout the design process to structure the intermedial relationships between digital scenography and the play. In this way, creative design and artistic processes continually intersect with philosophical inquiry in my approach to practice. Therefore, presenting this critical framework offers valuable insights for the subsequent analysis.

In her chapter *Parasitic Politics: Elfriede Jelinek's 'Secondary Dramas',* Karen Juers-Munby introduced Hans-Thies Lehmann's argument on the political possibilities of contemporary post-dramatic theatre. Lehmann advocated that theatre has to change to achieve its inherent political potential. He claimed that: '[a] repoliticisation of theatre can only be achieved if it does not accommodate itself to the order of representation but instead 'changes the form, the time and the space of the theatrical event'' (Lehmann in Juers-Munby, 2013: 209). Following Derrida's argument, Lehmann claimed that this *changed theatre* would 'let in other voices that do not get heard and that have no representation within the political order, and in this way open the site of theatre for the political outside' (in Juers-Munby, 2013: 210).

I feel that the need for a *changed theatre* resonates with both of the plays since at their core they deal with themes of change and transformation, where identity itself as author Rabey claims, 'is not fixed' and his plays 'depict attempts to break some fatalistic, deterministic cycle of inherited values and self-partitioning' (Rabey, in this volume: 147). The texts also give voice to the marginalised and the disenfranchised within our society, setting their cause in opposition to the political order of late neo-liberal capitalism and its often-oppressive regimes of representation. As Lara Kipp argued in her essay for this volume, they expose the 'constructed nature' of these narratives 'by way of pluralistic interrogation' (Kipp, in this volume: 252). I contend that one of the plays' aims and ambitions is to re-politicise change. Therefore, I consider in what ways digital scenography can effectuate this in the context of the political potential of theatre as advocated by Lehmann.

How can it influence the theatrical event in light of Lehmann's postulate and propel the critical impetus of the productions beyond the order of representation? In this contextual exposé, I explore two theoretical starting points that served both as an inspiration and a model for the dramaturgical function of the digital scenographies during the design process: the concept of an 'assemblage' stemming from Rosi Braidotti's theories and Elfriede Jelinek's concept of a 'secondary play', theorised as a parasitic play by Karen Juers-Munby.

To begin with, I consider philosopher Rosi Braidotti's concept. Braidotti argued that in the posthuman age, subjects are assemblages in 'the process of becoming' that she called 'nomadic becoming' (2018: 2–3). She argued thus that, subject formation takes on the form of the 'in-between nature/technology; male/female; black/white; local/global; present/past – in assemblages that flow across and displace [these] binaries' (*ibid.*: 3) These notions have affinity with themes in both plays where characters such as Cai and Owain in *Land of My Fathers* and

Tanwen and Annie in *Last Ditch* undergo radical transformations in their non-heteronormative relationships, thus demonstrating according to Kipp, the 'politically transformative potential of queer desire in Rabey's two plays' (Kipp, this volume, 260). This act of queer transformative politics that Kipp identified within the two works also has an affinity with the 'in-between' subject formations where, according to Braidotti, assemblages have the potential to displace binaries that are so prevalent in dominant regimes of representation. This concept also resonates with the structure of Rabey's characters, which often take the form of a postmodern *bricolage*. As the author comments in the foreword to *Land of My Fathers*:

> [my] three characters [...] try to construct national affiliations and masculine identities through some frantic *bricolage* of the fragments they find: James Bond films, music, comics, popular culture, foundation myths, nihilistic detachment, hedonism, narcotics. (Rabey, in this volume: 147)

Braidotti's concept of the 'assemblage' greatly appealed to me since it helped me think through the play's postmodern multifaceted nature. It also became a structural metaphor that enabled me to think more practically about implementing a multi-layer structure in the digital scenography design to effectuate a transformative political rupture of the material at hand. Thus, in this chapter I use Braidotti's concept of the 'assemblage' as a framework to discuss the overall multi-layered aspect of the 'digital scenography' in the two pieces—a 'digital scenographic assemblage'—one that engenders the notion of 'nomadic becoming' and creatively disrupts dominant political discourses of late capitalism that both plays critique. This theoretical paradigm is used in conjunction with Elfriede Jelinek's concept of the 'secondary play', with which Braidotti's theories have many affinities. Also, may the reader note that I will use the terms 'digital scenography' and 'digital scenographic assemblage' interchangeably.

Where Braidotti's concepts offer a theoretical starting point to think about and discuss the structural aspects of the digital scenography, Austrian playwright and novelist's, Elfriede Jelinek concept of a 'secondary play' ('parasitic play') (Juers-Munby, 2013: 211) offers a theoretical starting point and conceptual model to focus on the relationship and even the relationality between the two plays and their respective digital scenographic assemblages.

To discuss how this concept can be transferred and applied to a 'digital scenographic assemblage' logics, I will briefly introduce it here. A 'secondary play' is a play that is performed and staged concurrently and alongside another play (its 'host'), functioning as a critical juxtaposition and a form critical interference, a '*parallel (inter-)textuality*'. Two examples of productions of Jelinek's plays discussed by Juers-Munby, which use this dramaturgy of parallel intertextualities to effectuate a feminist critique, are*: Abraumhalde* (2009), a critique of Lessing's *Nathan the Wise,* and *FaustIn and Out* (2012), a critique of Goethe's *Faust.*

Juers-Munby expands on the concept of a 'parasitic' relationship between the 'host' play and the 'parasite'. She begins by considering three meanings of the term parasite:

> [f]irst, the social parasite who exploits the hospitality of others; secondly the biological parasite who feeds on another organism and weakens it... and thirdly... a form of static or interference that is noise on the channel of communication. (2013: 216)

Thinking through this quote, we can ask how to translate this into a dramaturgical agenda for the 'secondary', 'parasitic play'? What is dramaturgically at stake in this metaphor? From the first meaning, we can note that a 'parasitic play' is essentially an alien to its 'host'; welcome or not, it is there and will exploit its 'host's' 'hospitality'. It might use and refashion the ideas present in the 'host', its characters, themes, and tropes in a potentially exploitative and irreverent manner. From the second meaning, we can note that it will 'feed' on its material through intertextualities, allusions, and parallels, and it might feed deep, especially if the original 'host' is already full of intertextualities of other plays and cultural texts, the parasite will launch its tendrils to metastasize and drain its 'hosts' creative energies. From the third meaning, we can note that a 'parasitic play' will interfere with the material of the 'host'. It will also disrupt and challenge the clarity of the channel of communication through creative noise. It will jar and juxtapose ideas of the 'host' in creative and disruptive ways, with respectful disrespect.

So, how can we apply this metaphor and concept of a 'parasitic play' to the logic of a scenographic design? Also, importantly, who would be the 'hosts' in the case of the two plays? Would they be the plays themselves, their productions, or the intertextual material and socio-political contexts that underlie them?

To answer the first question, one of the key aspects of Jelinek's concept that springs to mind when thinking about scenography is the notion of autonomy. The idea of a scenographic design as a separate, autonomous entity, one that I shall argue is politically 'parasitic' in these productions, is in tandem with other discourses on the role of scenography in contemporary performance. For example, Neill O'Dywer quotes Sodia Lotker and Richard Gough to argue that scenography is not a mere setting for a performance but 'a body (a discipline, a method, a foundation) in its own right. It is a discipline that has its own logic, its own distinctive rules' (in Lotker and Gough, 2013: 3). He further quotes Scott Palmer and Joslin McKinney, who advocate this view and argue that 'scenography [is] not simply […] a by-product of theatre but […] a mode of encounter and exchange founded on spatial and material relations between bodies, objects and environments' (in McKinney and Palmer, 2017: 2). Thus, scenography is 'an environment, a world to be experienced, engaged and encountered kinaesthetically, physically and viscerally' (O'Dywer, 2023: 11).

In terms of the second question, who in this case are the hosts, how I will frame the analysis will consider the 'hosts' to be both the plays themselves and the underlying socio-political contexts and intertextualities that the plays themselves critique. This may initially seem like a conjectural chain of critical disruption, but this is also the case with Jelinek's 'parasitic plays' that are performed on top of 'classical' texts. These texts were and, in some ways, still are considered critiques and disruptions of the then status quo. For instance, Goethe's *Faust*, 'in its sprawling, stylistically heterogenous 'self-reflexive playfulness', has been called 'proto-postmodern' (in Juers-Munby, 2013: 231). So perhaps in the case of the two productions I will examine in this chapter, the parasitic digital scenography, can be seen as a 'thermal exciter' as Juers-Munby puts it, an intruder that '*modo obliquo* releases the political dynamite' (ibid) contained in the original plays, allowing for an experience of the political as disruption, a re-politicizing 'rupturing of the present' (ibid).

Thus, inspired by Elfriede Jelinek's concept of the 'secondary play' and taking into account the arguments buttressed by Lotker, Gough, Palmer, McKinney and O'Dywer, the digital scenographic assemblage could be seen as a form of a concurrent performance/experience that runs alongside a 'host' play. It is neither a supportive accompaniment in any traditional sense nor a passive one in how it functions dramaturgically. Instead, it engages with the performance and its other elements in some of the following ways: (1) it visually juxtaposes ideas enabling iconoclasm, parody, critique and satire; (2) it re-contextualises scenarios, morphing, recombobulating existing material; (3) it makes critical political commentaries through juxtapositions and creative disruptions; (4) and establishes a network of correspondences and intertextualities that enmesh the performance through interference. This is not an extensive list of effects that a parasitic scenography may engender. Still, it is a starting point and can serve as a framework to think critically and creatively about its dramaturgical function.

With these theoretical frameworks in mind, I move on to the analysis of the first case study, *Land of My Fathers. Land of My Fathers* is a politically charged drama that explores national identity, historical memory, queer masculinity, and post-colonial imperialist contexts in what appears to be at first glance a very loose parallel to the *Heart of Darkness* a.k.a. *Apocalypse Now* narrative trope. The story concerns three British ex-soldiers who have been contracted by 'The Chief'—a grey eminence from within the annals of the MI6—to go on a paramilitary mission to Afghanistan and Iraq as undercover spies to investigate alleged shifts in loyalties amongst their colleagues and to find out whether some of them have 'gone native'. The play juxtaposes their personal narratives with larger political struggles, the impact of global late capitalism and neo-liberalism on a war-torn Middle East, the commercialization of modern warfare, and concerns over Welsh national and cultural identity within the broader context of British identity.

In *Land of My Fathers*, the live action on stage was set against a projection backdrop that consisted of animations running concurrently with the live performance. From a scenographic standpoint, the projection screen comprised the space of the digital scenography. The digital element occupied that space.

Throughout the performance, the projections utilized mixed-media approaches, such as charcoal and ink drawings, digital painting, 3D animation, and videography, to construct a visually dense scenographic landscape (Fig. 1).

(Fig. 1: animation of flight to Afghanistan, with live actors in front, from the left: Russell Gomer, Oliver Morgan-Thomas and Huw Blainey. Photo: Keith Morris)

In tandem with the concept of a 'parasitic scenography', for the most part, the projections did not illustrate the action nor oversignify the context of the play and its scenes but actively disrupted, commented upon, and recontextualized the dramatic material. By introducing intertextual references and visual counterpoints, the digital scenography challenged dominant narratives and enabled a critical engagement with the play's themes by becoming a parasitic element in the performance. To analyse this relationship more closely and considering the theoretical frameworks, I look at (1) neo-cinematic intertextualities, (2) myths and metaphors, and (3) abject sensualities.

Neo-Cinematic Intertextualities

The digital scenography employs a 'neo-cinematic aesthetic' by absorbing and transforming cinematic forms, creating a mosaic of interwoven filmic references and juxtaposing their context with that of the play. Drawing on Julia Kristeva's notion that 'any text is constructed as a mosaic of quotations' (Kristeva 1986: 37), the scenographic design integrates imagery reminiscent of films such as *Apocalypse Now*, *The English Patient*, *Hurt Locker*, *Full Metal Jacket, Black*

Hawk Down and the *James Bond* franchise to name a few. These intertextual references contribute to a sense of historical layering, reinforcing the play's themes of war, trauma, and fragmented identity. The play opens with an Exordium, a series of animation vignettes/scenes framed through the famous barrel of the gun image that doubles as a camera shutter to separate the scenes (Fig. 2-3*). The scenes refer to visual tropes and scenarios from James Bond films. Composed in a surreal, parody-like, comic book style, each little scene comprises some failure, mishap, or accident, where the 'James Bond' character (played by Przemek Sobkowicz) 'fails' to live up to the famous agent's 'epic image'.

(Fig. 2 Exordium animation)

More importantly, however, he fails to embody the 'impossible' cinematic tropes and scenarios and the multiplicity of settings that he is thrown into by the relentless montage of the gun barrel *cum* camera shutter. This is emphasised by the fact that the animations are crafted CGI and carry a 3D cartoony aesthetic. Sobkowicz is a live recording composited as a videography layer, creating an ontological juxtaposition and, consequently, a 'distanciation' effect. There is also a live physicalisation of some of Sobkowicz's movements by the three live performers on stage, which again reinforces the impossibility of the embodiment of cinematic illusions crafted on the screen and the fragmentary nature of montage. From the outset, there is a sense of fragmentation of identity and identity as a postmodern multiplicity, a bricolage. This has affinity with one of the play's themes, which sees the protagonists trying to 'desperately, pathetically, endearingly, foolishly [...] construct' (Rabey, in this volume: 147) a sense of integrated (Welsh) cultural identity and instead ending up resorting to superficial, often cinematic/ pop cultural tropes and 'camp' (Sontag 1964: 515) substitutes.

Thus, from the very beginning, the digital scenography initiates a parasitic relationship with the dramatic material at hand, by constructing a multilayered assemblage, which 'feeds off' various levels of intertextuality and critically addresses dramaturgical tensions and self-reflexive themes that will develop throughout the play.

It is worth mentioning here how the digital scenography employs intertexts and ironic juxtapositions of visual tropes from Hollywood war films, which serve to foreground and critique imperial Western ideology by foregrounding the 'politics of perception' and 'response-ability' (Lehmann, 2006: 185, transl. Karen Juers-Munby) behind their cinematic forms. Lehmann reminds us that theatre should not focus on the content of the political message but rather foreground the form through which it is presented to elicit the spectator to question and position themselves politically in relation to the material. An example of this would be the allusions to Ridley Scott's *Black Hawk Down*, which focuses on a group of American soldiers on a mission in Somalia, their inner lives and struggles, and ultimately romanticised deaths that are given extensive screen time montage. At the same time, about a thousand Somalians who were killed during the operations are framed as 'cannon fodder' deaths and filmed ('shot') in a manner reminiscent of a first-person shooter video game. Again, through intertextualities, juxtapositions, and the use of a mixed-media approach of CGI and charcoal animation, the digital scenography feeds and provocatively disrupts the political contexts of the play.

(Fig. 4 Russell Gomer as Iestyn set against a charcoal/CGI animation of a Black Hawk. Photo: Keith Morris)

Lastly, I would like to discuss the imagery of the cave. The projection begins with a descent through a tunnel. As Kipp points out, this scene is a metaphor for the descent into the underworld, the *katabasis*. The tunnel is a dark, twisted, moist cave with a disturbingly organic quality. As such, its imagery resonates with the concept of the entanglement of the drives of *eros* and *thanatos* that have been discussed as an integral part of this journey by Kipp, where Cai and Owain encounter the possibility of a future queer relationship, or in Braidotti's words, a 'process of becoming' (Braidotti, 2018: 2). The inside of the cave was inspired by the cave wall paintings from the Cave of Swimmers in the Glif Kebir plateau, painted c. 8000 BC. They are famously featured in Anthony Minghella's *The English Patient* (1996), where the caves are also a site of *eros* and *thanatos*. That is where Catherine and Almasy, the two protagonists of the movie, consolidate their romantic relationship. Eventually, it is also where Catherine is left to die after a plane accident, with her death subsequently leading to a sequence of events that ends with Almasy's demise. The digital scenography projection in the cave shows three apparitions that emerge out of a cascading wall of sand. The first one is as Owain describes: …three massive horses, entwined, frozen frantic in the act of devouring each other. The second 'the Spirit of Defeat', as Cai puts it: 'It's an anatomical model that used to be in a surgeons' college. [Scratch] added the wings and helmet, I modified the arms an' face' and the third: 'Santa Muerte', Death itself.

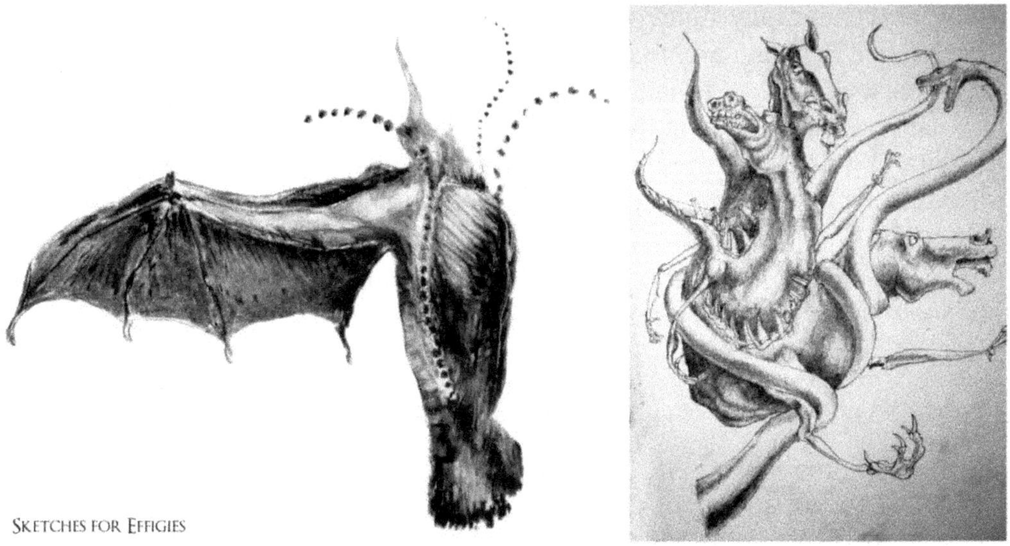

(Fig. 5 drawings of Effigies by Piotr Woycicki for the apparition's animation)

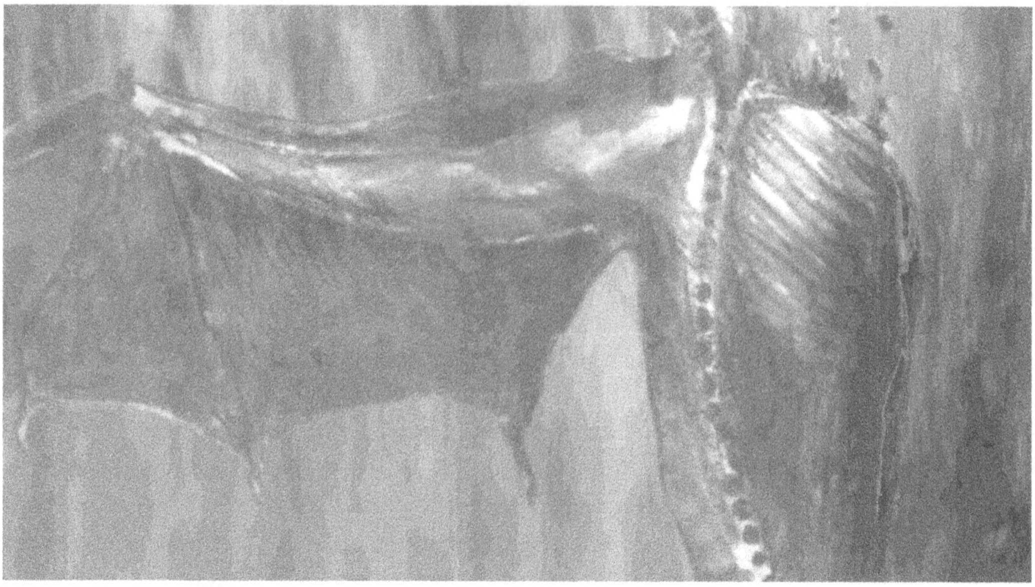

(Fig. 6 Effigies within the Wall of Sand animation)

They are followed by an animation of illuminated charcoal drawings featuring imagery previously present in the piece, such as scenes of Abu Ghraib torture and sketches of post-war ruins from Iraq and other Middle Eastern areas affected by the second Gulf War conflict[1].

The digital scenography functions as an assemblage of layers and intertextualities, subverting and resisting a potentially romantic interpretation of the scene, 'a violent divestment from romanticised notions of a heteronormative, male-coded Welsh nationalism' (Kipp, in this volume: 255). It also brings in a political commentary, pointing to the imperial context of Western occupation of the Middle East. Both contexts exist in the play and in the romantic and post-colonial themes of *The English Patient*. The parasitic character of the scenography compounds and interferes with the play and its filmic intertexts, opening up aporetic possibilities for interpretation and critique.

Myths and Metaphors

The digital scenography also engages with mythological and symbolic imagery, drawing from classical myths such as the Minotaur and the Abduction of Europa[2]. There are references to the Minotaur in the play, such as 'the minotaur of anticipation squatting in the maze of logic' (Rabey foreword: 147), and I extended them to form a metaphorical layer, which pervaded the piece. According to the

[1] For the full animation please see Fig. 7* on the website.

[2] Please see *Abduction of Europa (1623)* by Rembrandt van Rjin for reference.

ancient Greek myth, the Minotaur is a hybrid creature, born out of violation and one that perpetuates violence. He is both a victim and perpetrator, collapsing and blurring the binary distinction between these two positions. When visually implementing the figure of the minotaur, I considered intertexts such as Damien Hirst's 2017 exhibition at Venice Biennale, *Treasures from the Wreck of the Unbelievable* and works by Pablo Picasso. References to Minotaur iconography feature throughout the digital scenography and reinforce themes of entrapment, hybridity, and identity negotiation, echoing Braidotti's notion of the 'in-between' state of subject formation. This symbolic layering also blurs the lines between past and present, legend and lived experience. One way this manifests itself is through images on a spinning urn—an ancient storytelling device—which changes images every time it turns like in a comic book strip[3].

(Fig. 9 Images of torture on a spinning urn)

I drew sketches of Minotaurs torturing prisoners based on images of the atrocities perpetrated by guards from the Abu Ghraib prison.

[3] For the full animation, please see Fig. 8* on the website.

(Fig. 10 Minotaur sketches by Piotr Woycicki)

(Fig. 11 Minotaur sketches by Piotr Woycicki)

The urn appears during the mission debrief given to the contractors by 'The Chief'. During that scene, the chief also espouses the political context of the regions they are being sent to, implicitly stating that these areas' imperial capitalist Western occupation resulted in their social and economic destitution. As such, the digital scenography interferes with and comments upon these contexts, bringing in new layers of meaning and merging ancient forms of visual communications, urns, with their contemporary CGI manifestation.

The Minotaur also appears in more surprising and satirical contexts within the animations, complicating, blurring and also undermining its preestablished logics, making his metaphoric logic within the piece labyrinthian. When juxtaposed with live actions, he sometimes appears incongruous, comically disturbing, and at times upstaging the actors, becoming a jesting 'static interference'.

(Fig. 12 Minotaur 'squatting in the labyrinth' Oliver Morgan-Thomas as Owain, Russell Gomer as Iestyn, photo: Keith Morris)

(Fig. 13 Dancing Minotaur, Huw Blainey as Cai, Oliver Morgan-Thomas as Owain, photo: Keith Morris)

According to Roland Barthes, myth is a second-order semiological system 'which has the pretension of transcending itself into a factual system' (Barthes in Schaffer 1998: 41), a fictitious construct that passes itself for a fact. He goes on to argue that:

> In passing from history to nature, myth acts economically: it abolishes the complexity of human acts. It gives them the simplicity of essences, […], it establishes a blissful clarity: things appear to mean something by themselves.(1973: 156)

Arguably, implementing the Minotaur throughout the digital scenography complicates and disrupts the integrity of the myth as a second-order semiological system that Barthes discusses, deepening and igniting the political charge of the piece. By juxtaposing allusions to the myth of the Minotaur with contemporary political imagery, the digital scenography disrupts the myth-making processes that often sanitize national imperialist narratives, confronting the audience with historical and ongoing violence. Thus, the Minotaur can be seen as a 'parasite' in a tripartite meaning of the term, one that overstays his welcome and exploits hospitality, one that 'feeds' on the materials of the 'host' and one that disrupts and interferes with the 'host's' performance.

Abject Sensualities

The digital scenography also disrupts and interferes with the meaning-making process by implementing visceral abject imagery. In *Powers of Horror (1982),* Julia Kristeva describes the abject as 'what disturbs identity, system, order' (1982: 4), a force that resists categorization and threatens meaning itself. She argues that:

> The abject has only one quality of the object—that of being opposed to I. If the object, […] settles me within the fragile texture of a desire for meaning, […] what is *abject,* […] draws me toward the place where meaning collapses. (1982: 1)

In *Land of My Fathers*, in the ambush scene, Kipp argues that Cai and Owain exhibit a 'desire for self-annihilation by way of ecstatic union with a radically different other' (this volume: 254). The *other*, in the context of this scene, is potentially death itself or an encounter with death. Death is an abject *other* par excellence, an abject encounter that drains all meaning like an asymptotic approach to a collapsing star. The projection for this scene displayed a giant beating heart, slowly morphing and deforming beyond figurative recognition[4].

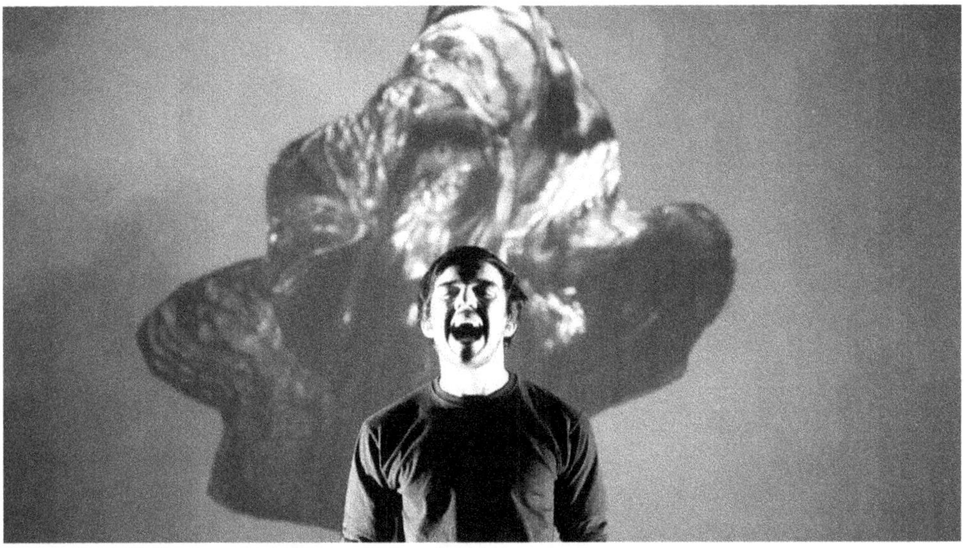

(Fig. 15 Heart animation Huw Blainey as Cai, photo: Keith Morris)

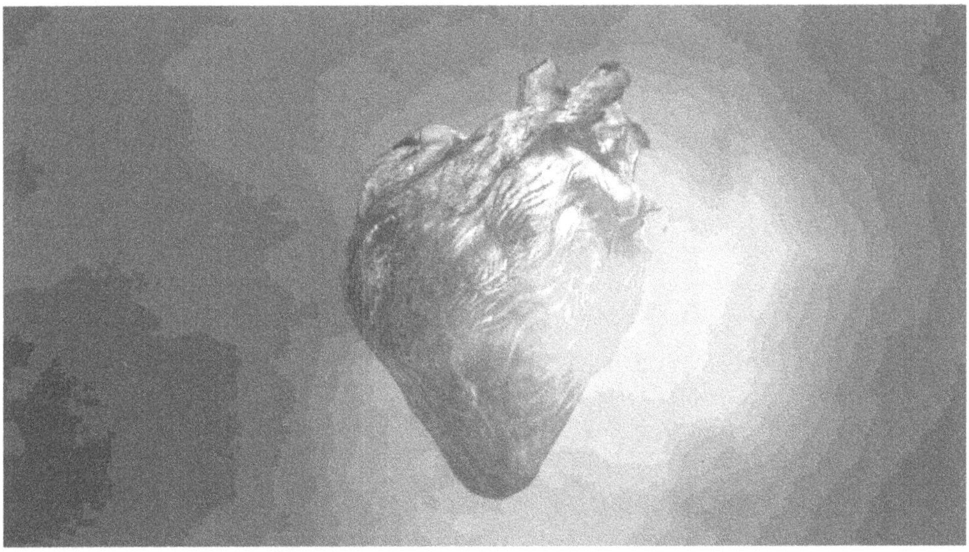

(Fig. 16 Heart animation)

On a superficial level, the animation could be interpreted as representing an amplified vital organ under strain during an intense combat action. The digital

[4] For the animation, please see Fig. 14 on the website.

scenography exposed a hodological space, a haptic internal space, a space of disorientation, and a space to be felt rather than externally optically apprehended. As the heart morphed, it became abject, a place where meaning is slowly dismantled, but a place to which one is, nonetheless, sensually drawn. In those disorienting moments, the digital scenography became an assemblage of abject sensualities and a parasitic element reconfiguring the experiential momentum of the host's mise-en-scene by collapsing the bodily outside of the live actors on stage with the bodily inside of the heart's anatomy.

Having analysed and reflected upon the function of the digital scenography in *Land of My Fathers* I will now turn to *Last Ditch*, which has a different scenographic design and assemblage structure. It also engenders and explores different aspects of the parasitic dynamic in relation to its host.

Last Ditch

The narrative explores themes of oppression, resistance, and transformation, set against a backdrop of societal and cosmic conflicts. It begins with the brutality of state power, where peaceful protests are met with violence, and individuals are tortured for their beliefs. This oppression leads to intense personal suffering, addiction, and betrayal, highlighting the destructive impact of authoritarian control on both victims and enforcers[5].

The scenographic design of *Last Ditch* comprised an oval space with walls made up of strands of cloth (Fig. 17).

(Fig. 17 A 3D sketch of the scenographic design by Richard Downing/Piotr Woycicki)

[5] For a full synopsis, please see Rabey, in this volume: 1-3.

This made all the walls 'permeable', like a giant porous membrane, and allowed the performers to move through the walls, on and off stage. The two ends of the oval structure functioned as projection screens.

(Fig. 18 performance space for *Last Ditch*, photo: Piotr Woycicki)

Much as with *Land of my Fathers*, the projections and animations of mixed-media run throughout the whole piece. Techniques used were charcoal and ink drawings, digital painting, motion graphics, 3D animation, videography, 3D sculpture, and modelling. I also introduced photogrammetry, a technique I have not used before, to capture some of the statues and to produce an accurate 3D model of Meri Well's *Lynx,* a golem-like creature that features in the piece's pivotal moment.

One of the design choices I made for this piece was to increase the use of 3D models and CGI. As such, this required me to create many 3D assets and models that could be employed at various moments throughout the piece. Most of the models and animations were created in Adobe Aftereffects (Motions graphics, compositing program), Blender (3D modelling and animation package) and ZBrush (3D sculpting program).

Below are some examples of the 3D models, 'assets' created for the piece. Many of the designs feature in the Lynx's speech scene, which is a 23 min animation (available on the website) in which Lynx reanimates artworks and statues that then cause havoc across the world. Hence, many of the designs allude to artworks such as those of Damien Hirst – *Treasures from the Wreck of the Unbelievable* (2017), Alfie Bradley—*Knife Angel* (2018*),* Meri Wells—*The Lynx* and Mario Rutelli's *Aberystwyth War Memorial* to name a few. I will discuss the Lynx's speech in more detail later on.

In many cases, I decided to fragment and fracture the statues and use graffiti as a way to both vandalise and create layers of intertextuality. These aesthetics were in tandem with the logic of 'parasitic' strategies discussed in the previous case study, adding additional layers of meaning and instilling self-reflective framings to the statues. In this sense the models themselves became parasites of their referent artwork hosts.

(Fig. 19 Harpies 3D models)

(Fig. 20 Lynx 3D model)

On several occasions, Rutelli's statues appear in the piece. I redesigned them to make them appear as fragmented, corroded and crumbling to critically undermine their apparent romanticised and neo-classical sensual aesthetic. Rutelli's statues come from a War Memorial in Aberystwyth that honours the victims of the First and Second World Wars. I find it very unsettling and hypocritical that an artist like Rutelli who was heavily sponsored and endorsed by Benito Mussolini throughout his career, designed these war memorial statues. He designed a memorial to commemorate the fallen in wars that were initiated by the very regime that sponsored his career. It is almost as if the statues carry a hidden controversy within them, a political dissonance. It is this sense of irony, dissonance, and disruptive juxtaposition that I wanted the parasitic scenographic to bring out and make provocatively explicit also on the level of model design. A parallel might be drawn here with a scene from the Lynx's Speech, discussed later, where a re-animation of The Marmi Boys statues occurs, as Rabey put it 'subverted and released into their latent but innate 'raging queerness'', and thus highlighting the hypocrisy of Mussolini's fascist regime that was openly homophobic.

(Fig. 21 Aberystwyth War Memorial animation)

(Fig. 22a and Fig.22b Re-design of the Rutelli statues, charcoal drawings by Piotr Woycicki)

In the following section, I look at different aspects of the digital scenography and focus on specific instances within the piece to analyse the function of the parasitic scenographic. The digital scenography had lots of strands and layers that comprised the scenographic assemblage. These layers intertwined and were entangled with each other, creating a mesh of intertextualities and associations throughout the piece. In this section, I will consider five strands with distinct dramaturgical function and thematic contexts: (1) parallel (inter)textualities, (2) soul shards, (3) surreal allusions, (4) location contexts and (5) movie-within-a-play, 'The Lynx Speech'.

Strand I: parallel (inter)textualities

Throughout the piece, there were several scenes where the digital scenography deepened and foregrounded layers of intertextuality in similar ways to the *Land of My Fathers*. One of these scenes comes halfway through the play, where the protagonist Tanwen is released from prison, and one of the 'supernaturals', Annie, materializes before her. Annie gives Tanwen an overview of the events so far before exhorting her to form a resistance. In order to accompany the 'debrief', I decided to use a similar technique I used in *Land of My Fathers*, a spinning object with an imprinted pictorial 'story'. Instead of an urn, however, I opted for a cauldron, namely *The Gundestrup Cauldron*, dated 150 BC (Fig. 23).

(Fig. 23 *The Gundestrup Cauldron,* photo: Knud Winckelmann and Nationalmuseet)

The cauldron is associated with the myth of Bran the Blessed, who was an intertext for the character of Annie. Much like the urn, it also became a formal storytelling device and echoed Lehmann's emphasis on formal manipulation as a method for re-politicisation in theatrical presentation. I decided to juxtapose Annie's debrief with references to historical instances of protest and demonstration representations, ranging from recent Black Lives Matter to Francisco Goya's *Disasters of War*. To illustrate part of the process of creating the intertextual imagery, I re-imagined and pastiched some of Goya's works by drawing charcoal versions of them in order to bring in contemporary contexts.

Third of May 1808 was transformed into a contemporary protest scenario, foreshadowing the final scene of *Last Ditch* and the type of protests Tanwen has been privy to thus far.

(Fig. 24 Charcoal pastiche of Francisco Goya's *Third of May 1808 (1814)* by Piotr Woycicki)

(Fig. 25 Pastiche of Goya's *Azmodea, Fantastic Vision (1820)*) with references to climate change crisis by Piotr Woycicki)

(Fig. 26 Pastiche of Goya's *The Colossus (*1808*)* foreshadowing the upcoming catastrophe by Piotr Woycicki)

(Fig. 27 an example of how these images featured in the animation of the cauldron[6])

Through these intertextualities, the parasitic elements of the scenography functioned as a way to 'interfere' with the 'hosts' contexts and expand upon them. At times, challenging them but also 'igniting' the already present political impetus of the scene.

Strand II: Soul shards

Another strand in the assemblage of the digital scenography were shards. They were a visual trope throughout the piece, which featured in a number of ways. Graphically, they were 3D models of stained-glass shards that contained pre-recorded filmed sequences of characters' faces and their reactions towards the live delivery of the text and the mise-en-scene of the 'host' play in general. The shards usually appeared when a character was about to die and accompanied the speech that Boneblack would deliver at the point of a character's passing—when 'they 'break black' from their last moments'. An example of such a scene would be the appearance of Boneblack after Beti euthanises Joe, and Boneblack's speech as he 'releases' Joe's memories.

---

[6] The full animation can be accessed from the website see Fig. 28.

(Fig. 29 A shard with Joe's faces inside: N13)

Joe's face inside the shard would react to Boneblack's speech, adding a subtextual layer to the performance and often expressing a counterpoint to what was being said. As such it formed what Isabella Pluta defined as a 'mediaphoric body'. Pluta defines the 'mediaphoric body' as follows: '[f]rom an etymological perspective, this concept incorporates three elements of a different order, both concrete and conceptual: the living, the media-related and the metaphorical' (2010: 193).

If applied to this scene, then the 'mediaphoric body', becomes a complex amalgam of live performance (in this case the live performance of Boneblack and Joe's live presence on stage), the mediated performance (Joe's facial expressions inside the shard) and the metaphorical compound character that results from it (a multiple fragmented impression of Joe's character). A similar implementation of the shards was used during Ronan's and Sion's deaths.

Another example would be Dyfrig's monologue in the first part of the play[7]. This example was also interesting because it contained a 'multiplicity' of facial expressions and reactions juxtaposing them against each other. This simultaneous manifestation of subtexts resonated with what Lehmann has defined as 'simultaneity' (Lehmann, 2006: 87)—a staging of multiplicity of perspectives which foregrounds the 'fragmentary character of perception' (*ibid*).

[7] See Fig. 30 on the website.

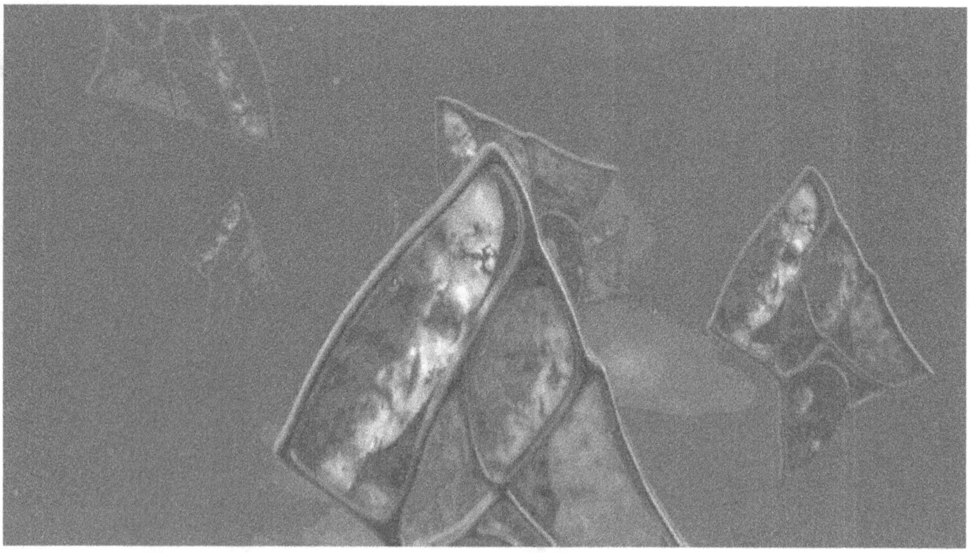

(Fig. 31 Dyfrig's shards: C3)

At times, the shards formed shapes like that of a skull during Tanwen's monologue after the interrogation.

(Fig. 32 Tanwen's monologue: N10)

Through the implementation of the shards trope, the digital scenography added a layer of subtext to the performances that was not present in the 'host's' live performance by making internal psychological spaces visually manifest themselves within a surreal aesthetic of a floating shard. Through these reconfigurations and responses to live performance, the parasitic elements of the scenography functioned as a way to expand but also potentially question and undermine what was being said. For example, Boneblack's speeches attempted to summarise a person's life memories in a few paragraphs, an impossible task and a testament to the limitations of language itself. Thus, in this case, the shards in the digital scenography provided a critical lens that elicited the audience to question the truth value of what was being said and also the form and the very medium of language through which these 'memory facts' were being delivered.

Strand III: Surreal allusions

Another strand, in the assemblage of the digital scenography were the surreal allusions. These were animations that were juxtaposed with the live action of the 'host'. Some examples would be an animation of a skull being crushed in slow motion during the protest scene.

(Fig. 33 Protests scene: N6)

(Fig. 34 Tanwen's interrogation scene: N8)

(Fig. 35 Ronan's suicide scene: A4)

This strand of digital scenography created a mesh of metaphors that loosely resonated with the host's material, opening up possibilities for interpretation but also changing the sense of temporality. By slowing time, it arguably intensified the dramatic moments, at times literally opening up a wound, a temporal cesura, and presenting the scene within a temporal frame that demands more intense attention. As a parasitic element, it interfered with the live temporality of the host, disrupting its temporal frame. Thus, following Lehmann's advocacy for a need to re-politicise theatre, the digital scenography functions to '[change] the form, the time and the space of the theatrical event'' (Lehmann in Juers-Munby 2013: 209), foregrounding the 'politics of perception' of the theatrical moment beyond the immediate representation.

Strand IV: location contexts.

The digital scenography also functioned as a means of setting up The Lynx's Speech. This was perhaps less of a critical dramaturgical function and more of an 'establishing shot' dramaturgical function[8]. A particularly compelling setting is Wearhead's fortress. In the plot, the supernatural M, disdainful of humanity and its corruption, seeks to hasten its 'cosmic suicide.' To do so, he intervenes in human affairs by striking a Faustian bargain with Wearhead, an influential politician, granting him short-term dominance in exchange for his complicity. Suspended in space above the Earth, Wearhead's fortress is a floating cube from which he observes and monitors the world below. Within the fortress, smaller cubes spin and reconfigure, assembling mosaics and *bricollages* of media fragments transmitted from Earth. This ever-shifting surveillance mechanism echoes Foucault's concept of the panopticon, reinforcing the theme of omnipresent observation and control[9].

(Fig. 38 Inside Wearhead's fortress: A5)

---

[8] See Fig. 36* on the website.
[9] See Fig. 37* on the website.

The fortress also alludes to a Rubik's cube, where the fragmented representation of political contexts, mediated through the press, is transformed into a game. In this sense, the digital scenography design suggests that capitalist politicians like Wearhead manipulate public perception, distorting and reshaping historical events at will through a sophisticated game of media deception. In many ways, Wearhead functions as a parasite within the play, thriving at the expense of the global population. Thus, the digital scenography not only highlights Wearhead's parasitic nature but also underscores the mediums through which political agendas are shaped and contested on the world stage.

Strand V: Lynx's speech

The final strand/moment I would like to consider is the 'Lynx's Speech'. The speech comes at a point in the play when Anhrefn, aka Annie, guides Tanwen into a human summoning of The Lynx, 'Guardian doorman at the portal of the possible', to assist them in creating 'The Most Spectacular Event, In The History Of The World'. The Lynx materializes and stirs himself into triggering the simultaneous worldwide animation of statues, who rise up in opposition to various human forms of control and repression[10].

(Fig. 40 Scene from 'Lynx's Speech', R1, inspired by Jason DeCaires Taylor's *The Pride of Brexit*)

---

[10] For the full *Lynx's Speech* see Fig. 39* on the website.

The speech is a 23-minute animated film I made as part of the digital scenography that accompanied the text's delivery by Richard Lynch. It was a pivotal speech in the play where sculptures from around the world came alive to engage in an apocalypse of 'cosmic proportions'. The animated film functioned as a cinematic event, a film-within-a-play. and its inclusion in the piece was a bold, experimental move that exemplified many of the features and aspects of the parasitic scenographic discussed in the chapter thus far. Perhaps the most prominent was the exploitation of hospitality since it was a fairly long animation that interrupted the conventional flow of the play and made the audience watch an animated film as if they were in a cinematic setting. The speech was based on references to multiple artworks and thus heavily intertextual and self-referential in nature, which further emphasised its parasitic nature as discussed in this chapter.

The parasitic nature of the digital scenography in the piece carries the potential to creatively disrupt and illuminate the political contexts of the host. As Juers Munby remarks in relation to Jelinek's concept, it has the potential to 'allow us to perceive voices that often do not get represented' (Juers-Munby, 231). However, it also has the potential to open up avenues for economic and political dissent. In his book *Postcapitalism: A Guide to our Future* (2015), Paul Mason defines a new emergent economico-political order, that of 'postcapitalism'. The core of Mason's argument is that emerging technologies, particularly information technology, no longer align with the logic of neoliberal capitalist markets and cannot be commodified within the current capitalist system. He envisions future economic systems focused on information, where data and ideas replace material goods and monetary value as the primary means of exchange, which he terms postcapitalism. He identifies three key technological developments from the past twenty-five years that will make postcapitalism possible: the over-abundance of digital goods and information, the rise of collaborative production through expanding digital networks, and the progressive automation of production processes (Mason 2015: xv). In a world that is increasingly computerized, organised through A.I. and algorithms, and dominated by virtual modes of production, a parasitic 'Trojan horse' that could offer a mode of resistance and effectuate political change may very well come from the digital avant-garde. Much like a computer virus, digital artworks—and by extension 'parasitic scenographics'— could challenge the political agendas and affordances of the cultural mainstream frameworks—or what Roger Owen termed as 'hyperfacilitation' (Owen, this volume: 304) in his chapter for this volume. The digital can thus become the site of resistance and purposeful opposition to dominant regimes of representation. The 'political dynamite' that re-ignites the political potential of the 'host' it entangles itself with.

REFERENCES:

Barthes, Roland (2013*) Mythologies*, New York: Hill and Wang.

Braidotti, Rosi (2013) *The Posthuman*, Cambridge: Polity.

Chapple, Freda and Chiel Kattenbelt (2006) *Intermediality in theatre and performance*, New York: Rodopi.

Juers-Munby, Karen, Jerome Carroll and Steve Gilles (eds.) (2013) *Postdramatic Theatre and the Political*, London: Bloomsbury Methuen Drama.

Kristeva, Julia (1982) *Powers of horror: an essay on abjection*, New York: Columbia University Press.

Lehmann, Hans-Thies (2006) *Postdramatic Theatre*, trans. Jürs-Munby, London: Taylor and Francis.

Lotker, Sodja and Richard Gough (2013) 'On Scenography: Editorial', *Performance research* 18. No. 3: 3-6.

Mason, Paul (2015) *Postcapitalism: A Guide to our Future,* U.K.: Allen Lane.

Nelson, Robin (2013) *Practice as research in the arts: principles, protocols, pedagogies, resistances*, Basingstoke: Palgrave Macmillan.

O'Dwyer, Neill (2023*) Digital Scenography: 30 years of experimentation and innovation in performance and interactive media*, London: Methuen Drama.

Palmer and McKinney, Joslin and Scott Palmer (eds.) (2017) *Scenography expanded: an introduction to contemporary performance design* London: Bloomsbury Methuen Drama.

Pluta, Isabella (2010) 'Robert Lepage and Ex Machina, The Andersen Project (2005)' in Bey-Cheng, Sarah (et al), *Mapping intermediality in performance, Amsterdam*: Amsterdam University Press.

Sontag, Susan (1964). "Notes on 'Camp'". Partisan Review. 31 (4): 515–530.

Colston's Demise. Ink drawing by Piotr Woycicki

If Nietzsche Wrote Sitcom: Theatricality and Statuary in David Ian Rabey's *Land of my Fathers* and *Last Ditch (Anhrefn yng Nghymru)* by *Roger Owen*

Introduction

This edition of Rabey's latest plays is the third collection of his work to be published, following *The Wye Plays* (featuring *The Back of Beyond* and *The Battle of the Crows*) in 2004 and *Lovefuries* (*The Contracting Sea* and *The Hanging Judge*, along with the earlier *Bite or Suck*) in 2008. It adds to a body of work notable for its ferocious pursuit of articulacy, its joy in overt theatricality and its overwhelming faith in surprise and possibility. The two latest plays uphold those dramatic and theatrical principles, significantly developing them in a number of ways; and in that sense they are contentedly consistent with the previous work. But there are new and entirely unexpected things here too: exploratory forays into a quasi-naturalistic failure of language to articulate characters' distinctiveness; an interest in overtly Welsh identities, including incorporation of Welsh language wordplay and imagery; and – the features that are discussed at greatest length in this essay – an interest in statuary as an expression of and challenge to established socio-industrial norms, and the implicit deployment of comic structures.

Rabey's use of language in his plays has always been assertive and unabashedly distinctive. It is well known that some of the most important influences on his own writing have been writers such as Howard Barker and David Rudkin, both of whom, albeit in very different ways, use the language of their plays to a conscious and calculated theatrical effect rather than in pursuit of socially applicable realism. Following their examples, Rabey has tended to present characters who are boldly loquacious, and in situations where a skilled use of language is necessary to self-realisation, fulfilment or even survival. A pivotal point in all this is the fact that they do not necessarily know what they want until it forms in their mouths, startling them in the process and creating a confrontation with actuality which is not to be gainsaid. For example, Edgar in *The Back of Beyond*, having been bequeathed the final, summative lines of Shakespeare's *King Lear* – 'The oldest hath borne most; we that are young / Shall never see so much, nor live so long' (Shakespeare, 1994: 206) – as a starting point for his action, throws off the burden of Lear's overwhelming defeatism with a reckless 'UNLESS', from which the rest of the play must then issue. And Fury in *The Hanging Judge*, compelled by his own words to summon his abuser out from memory and up onto the stage, dispatches the Judge at the end via an instantaneously discovered rhythmic incantation which decisively if temporarily drives him out. Even characters such as Vixen in *The Battle of the Crows*, whose idiom of speech is an eloquently garbled hybrid FoxEnglish, seems insistent on her own garrulousness as a matter of anthrovulpinal pride: as with so many other characters, there's no stopping her.

The function of all this talk is to ensure that, whatever else the characters appear to be grappling with, one of their main concerns is with theatricality itself. Like the audience, the characters find themselves in the midst of something that is taking its course (to paraphrase Beckett in *Endgame*). Their awareness of their own role in engendering this theatricality may ebb and flow, but it is constantly available to them and can always be interrogated by them. In some cases, Rabey's characters find themselves consciously staging action either for the delectation or torment of their audience: in *The Back of Beyond*, for example, the overt theatricality of Edgar's speech to the marketgoers is followed by the nightmarish masque in which he himself is physically broken, and then by the cloying horror of Echternacht's staged delusion of familial life, out of which he breaks in murderous resolve to act. Similarly, and as already noted, both the plays in *Lovefuries* show the main character finding and articulating another presence inside them and thus being both actor and audience to their own troubling caprices. What is not in evidence here is a valorisation of constraint or a deterministic attitude to the way in which language might regulate theatricality. The plays, and Rabey himself, reject the premise of naturalism, in which dramatic characters' failure to articulate themselves through language engenders a subconscious, reflexive self-expression which remains tragicomically beyond their control.

The shadow of Shakespeare is cast across Rabey's work not only in relation to theatricality but also to its content. *The Wye Plays* are, of course, reactions to *King Lear*, but they are also overtly concerned with the matter of England and so sit in the Shakespearean tradition of tragedies and history plays. Again, Edgar in *The Back of Beyond* presents himself as a kind of warped John of Gaunt in his early speech specifying the target of his dissatisfaction: 'ENGLAND: land of wheezing hiatus, to be distinguished from its neighbours by its force of belief in yesterday or tomorrow, but never in today. The itch: to break its stride. Or let it break your own.' (Rabey, 2004: 17). Similarly, *The Battle of the Crows* concerns itself with a conflict between the Blacklands and the Marches, both identifiable as (largely) English territories. However, his latest plays present a departure from any exclusive concern with England, and fully and frenetically admit Wales and Welshness into their purview. Rabey has described *Land of My Fathers* as a 'rewilded' Welsh state of the nation drama (Rabey, this volume: 145); and *Last Ditch* goes even further by actively including Anhrefn/Annie's impulsive bilingualism (and multi-regional English) as a mockery of stricture. But neither play looks to be the focus of a journalistically amenable national debate, and both approach the treatment of nation with glorious and calculated itinerancy. Wales features as a location only for a small part of *Land of My Fathers*, and Welshness is subsequently offered up as a residual identity, a pool of assertions, practices and myths which enliven and trouble the characters' status and function as (*faux*) private contractors. Thus the playing on Welsh national tropes, myths and culturally ingrained skills occurs on a stage which has exploded and expanded beyond the horizon; and, along with most nations, Wales and Welshness is seen merely a residual cultural repertoire in an undifferentiated 'system of generalized exchange'. (Baudrillard, 2002: 9)

And *Last Ditch* spans almost every spatial dimension conceivable: from an elemental parallel universe, to an unlocated Welsh present, and thence to the specific (Aberystwyth) and even micro-local (dramatist's dining room). The consistency of focus which one might hope to see in a play reporting on the state of the nation is wholly absent, and the acquisition and application of signs of cultural difference completely overtaken by the extravagant play of hybrid possibility.

Statuary and Nietzschean laughter in *Land of My Fathers* and *Last Ditch*

Let us turn to the two new plays in a little more detail. No doubt that one of the main devices one finds in common between the two is the sudden, unexpected appearance and influence of statues on the dramatic characters and worlds which have been created. In *Land of My Fathers*, the secret which has been harboured throughout by the soldier/ security contractor Cai Thomas turns out to be an underground statue gallery, featuring grotesque versions of Duncan's Horses, Winged Victory and Death; and in *Last Ditch*, the intrigue wrought against the 'Mayflies' of humanity by the sinister figure M is stopped when public statues all over the world come to life and create sublime chaos in the streets. The intervention of statuary into the human world, suddenly dissolving the boundaries between the living and the dead, then, is a key device, upending character relationships and decentring the audience's sense of the dramatic world created by the plays.

The statues have the same function in both cases: simply and modestly, 'to overturn the dominant human terms of reality and consciousness'. And in both plays the intervention works, at least to the extent that one might be able to determine success or failure in a world utterly changed by the events in question. In *Land of My Fathers*, the surprise of finding and facing the underground effigies leads to a catastrophic break in trust between the three characters. The cynical and compliant Iestyn is murdered; after which, Cai and Owain suddenly find themselves in the throes of a previously unsuspected sexual passion. In effect, having experienced Death in the cave, first as a statuesque image and then as a real act, their bodies break out from an arrested posture resembling life, and into life itself. The key, says Owain, is to 'stop followin' orders'; but the whole change has already been precipitated by exposure to the art objects underground. These, says Cai (who, along with his mute uncle Scratch, has spent four years making them in secret), manifest 'the unspeakable principles of this world':

> We are manifestin': the unspeakable principles of this world.
> Fuck Redemption, 'greater good', crosses an'
> crucifixions. That's to reassure frightened kids.
> These show you the real deal.
> Human bein's break. They're DESIGNED to.
> They show the UTTER LOSS of CONTINUITY.
> There are stories that go on, beyond them.
> But they ain't told, or made, or understood: by
> anythin' that's human.
>
> (Rabey, this volume: 235-6)

These chthonic objects, created through breakage, showing the effects of breakage, themselves cause breakage in the characters and in the play itself.

In *Last Ditch*, the change wrought by the intervention of statuary is even more substantial in terms of its reach into the dramatic world of the play and into the manner of its theatrical presentation. The rebel Tanwen, fighting back against the system which has oppressed and disfigured her, meets the immortal elemental Anrhefn (working on Earth as Annie) and is consequently given the means to unleash 'The Most Spectacular Event, In The History Of The World!' This, somewhat bathetically it would seem, is to be created by 'The Lynx of Meri Wells', a ceramic figure in the possession of the dramatist, which the vast majority of the audience will have never seen and for which they will have no points of reference whatsoever. However, again, the intervention works. The Lynx appears and releases irresistible forces of change into an astonished world, using 'what HE alone KNOWS: t'summon the forces, spark the friction, make that crackshot deadeye penalty kick that will convert the fear into ASTONISHMENT' (Rabey, this volume: 106). This is a bold dramatic premise in itself, collapsing the play's discourse from dealing with a socially and politically identifiable world (albeit one modified by the intervention of god-like elemental forces) into an assertion of the power of an entirely obscure object. In production, as is reported at length in the present volume, this was further enhanced by suspending the live action and presenting The Lynx's intercession through Piotr Woycicki's 20-minute computer animation.

If this all sounds rather Nietzschean, then that's not much of a surprise. Transformation and change were central preoccupations in Nietzsche's thought, not only in terms of its content, where they could be seen as indicative of humanity's release from forces of superstition, fear and acquiescence, but also in its form as a body of work whose preoccupation with change is embodied by its complexity and tempestuous resistance to consistency. One of the Nietzsche's most significant texts from this point of view, *Thus Spoke Zarathustra*, posits two possible conditions for mankind: the *Übermensch*/Superman or The Last Man. The Nietzschean Superman is a figure elevated to greatness by having 'surpassed man', but he is held in that position only by a constant opposition to and struggle against forces which aim at his debasement. Attaining the desired but elusive status of Superman requires an act of transformation, a dedication to transcendence and a view of the condition thus achieved as being substantially different from the norm. Conversely, Last Man status is available by default to anyone who remains content as they are. Of course, what the exact terms of this transformation into Superman might entail – where and how you might become one, and how you'd know if you did – remain unclear (thankfully: this indefiniteness is one of the factors that helps to defend Nietzsche's work from accusations of outright supremacism and Fascism). However, what is clear is the sense of the Superman as an arresting figure, suspended between a self-transforming action and an iconic, self-denoting stillness.

That suspension between action and stillness is also exemplified by the figures discovered in the Iraqi tunnels in *Land of My Fathers*. They, too, work through creating an intense shock in the viewer – in this case, the other characters, since the statues are not shown to the audience – and the descriptions given of them indicate the implicit sense of motion, momentum and intent that co-exists with their petrified state. The first statue is of:

> OWAIN: …three massive horses, entwined, frozen frantic in the act of devouring each other. One is clambering on the other's back but being pushed upwards, off-balance, its head at a sickening angle as the other bites out its throat. The third, entangled, has its face thrust out between their legs, eyes blind with hopeless horror. On their necks and flanks, the stone flesh hangs off them: like awful, ragged flowers.
>
> IESTYN: They are bound round by serpents: wrapping them, squeezing and twisting them to bursting point. The knot of pain, tightening. These serpents have - wings? (Rabey, this volume: 232-3)

The horses' arrested movement conveys the madness of their implicit action but also stands as an invitation to break into it, to contemplate their form and thus to 'surpass' the statue's merely representative status (and it is interesting to note the different ways in which the two characters react to this contemplation: Owain, who will survive this episode, offers up an accompanying metaphor, whilst Iestyn, who will not, can only question what he's seeing). Of course, not only do the statues convey movement through stillness, they also propose an equivalence between the base sculptural matter and living – or at least semi-living – flesh. This is more clearly shown in the second statue described, the Spirit of Defeat, a travesty on the theme of winged victory. 'It holds out two forearms, brandishing stumps where there should be hands', a sliced and opened nose, eyes without eyelids, and a lipless jaw 'showing yellow teeth and fangs, transplanted from a huge dog' (*ibid*.: 234). Again, rather than allowing himself to bind with the figure in contemplation, Iestyn asks about the statue's material origins:

IESTYN: What the fuck? Is it a dummy – ?

CAI: It's an anatomical model that used to be in a surgeons' college. [Scratch] added the wings and helmet, I modified the arms an' face. (*ibid*.: 234)

It may well have *been* an anatomical model, but, being now proposed as an art object, the extent to which it can still be seen as such is open to question; as is the relationship between its base material and its transformed self. Can it be both at the same time? The Nietzschean view might well be yes; since the power of its (grotesque) transcendence lies in our awareness of its movement out of one condition and into another. The fact that it appears to have been cannibalised from previously wrought materials only emphasises that movement.

The final figure to be revealed in the Iraqi tunnel takes the treatment of statuary further still. After Iestyn offers a description of it – Death, Santa Muerte, a 'massive THING… crowned by a sort of tribal headdress', the skin flayed from its face, with 'deepset cunning eyes, and a jaw 'hinged in an open laughscream' with hands as 'upturned claws, accepting and demanding all'(*ibid*.: 234-5) – the function of these figures for Cai and his uncle Scratch is encapsulated. These are objects of worship, the secrets of the world, Cai says; and he returns to this place whenever he can to 'Rededicate' (*ibid*.: 235) himself to Death. Of course, such a rededication cannot be literally made to death, but only to a life in which death is fully acknowledged, and in which any sources of security and succour used to shield one from the full knowledge and experience of death-in-life are eschewed. Again, one can find parallels for this kind of knowledge in Nietzsche's Zarathustra, who, in bringing the gift of his wisdom to mankind, disputes and rejects the words of the Saint he meets on his way from the mountain top to the marketplace, and recommends that his audience 'remain true to the earth, and believe not those who speak unto you of superearthly hopes!' (Nietzsche, 2001: 3). And, true to his word, he later comforts a dying tightrope walker not with some sense of transcendental meaning but that he perished by the very danger that had so characterised his life (*ibid*.: 8).

For all this wisdom, however, Zarathustra is derided by the market-goers. They laugh at him, and show a marked preference for the prospect of living like the Last Man rather than as the Superman. Their laughter is seen as an expression of contempt, and their rejection of Zarathustra a tacit claim for the superiority of their baseness over his philosophical labour: in response, he declares to himself – as many a high-minded performer in mid-act – that 'they understand me not; I am not the mouth for these ears' (*ibid.*: 7). In this sense, then, laughter, particularly as an index of comedy, is contemptible. However, there are other forms of laughter, and other modes and effects of comedy. In *Land of My Fathers* alone, for example, there is parody (the mock James Bond-style opening, leading to gleefully terse descriptions of violence), farce (the outrageous training of Iraqi volunteer soldiers to sing in Iestyn's Male Voice Choir) and burlesque (how else to quantify the intervention of David Garland Jones's *Ain't Seen Ruthin Yet* into the action of the play?), among many others; none of which necessarily conform simply or submissively to the notion of mockery found in *Zarathustra*. In *Last Ditch*, too, any recognisable comic tropes and types are complicated by their context and by the characters' capricious manner of self-expression. This leads to a kind of laughter in Rabey's plays which is far more likely to be individual, reprehensible, subversive and/or unbidden than communal, unifying and co-ordinated: laughter as manifest in Barker's Theatre of Catastrophe, in Artaud's Theatre of Cruelty (see Barker, 1993: 33-4; Artaud, 1993: 31). And in Nietzsche, too: when Zarathustra sees a shepherd choking on a serpent which has latched onto the inside of his throat, he calls on him to bite off its head; whereupon the shepherd, relieved of the lethal threat, becomes 'No longer shepherd, no longer man – a transfigured being, a light-surrounded being, that laughed! Never on earth laughed a man as he laughed!' (Nietzsche, 2001, p.108). This laughter issues forth when the individual is taken through terror to the very edge of life, and beyond the point of being recognisably human.

This is a kind of laughter beyond comedy, associated with a moment of ultimate self-realisation, of liberation not only from ordinary kinds of fears and anxieties with which one might associate Freud's theory of laughter, but also from all previously understood senses of identity and history, which Pete A. Gunter (1968) sums up as Nietzsche's 'dread of the eternal recurrence' (503). And in that sense, the underground gallery in *Land of My Fathers* and the transformed world of rampant statuary in *Last Ditch* might both be seen as locations in which a new and inconceivable laughter issue forth, whose mould-breaking comedy may only be admitted after a full accession to the horrors within.

But then again…

If Nietzsche wrote Sitcom

All this might only be true of a world which provided some kind of resistance to the Nietzschean will; a world which needed to be wrought by a great effort of soul. Writing in the latter part of the nineteenth century, Nietzsche inhabited such a world and duly offered up his Zarathustra to it. However, if he were to re-emerge from the mists of time and of his catastrophic mental breakdown, he would find today a very different kind of milieu, characterised not by resistance but by hyperfacilitation, of informatics, digital search engines and large language models. His stuff having been already datascraped, along with all its attendant contextualisation and critique, he might discover (assuming that he'd paid the subscription fee) a new, smashed-together contemporary prophet – ChatZar – embodying not the will to power, but rather an inexhaustible, uncritical biddability. And so, both Nietzsche and Zarathustra 1.0 would find themselves out of a job, or at the very least relieved of all the tiresome graft associated with philosophising, and finally able to do what they'd always really wanted…

To write sitcom.

To their astonishment (no doubt), they'd find that their pilots had already been in production. For all the recourse to Nietzschean laughter that we find in *Land of My Fathers* and *Last Ditch,* their most striking feature in relation to the rest of Rabey's *oeuvre* is the extent to which the usual pursuit of surprising enlightenment seems happy to co-exist with a reduction either in the circumstances of the action or of the purposefulness of its focus. And this reduction is congruent with some of the major features of sitcom. One of the most important of these, as Mintz (1985) argues, is the capacity of the main situation to regenerate itself, for the 'cyclical nature of the normalcy of the premise [to undergo] stress or threat of change and [be] restored' (114-5). More so than in Rabey's previous work, we find in these latest plays situations whose most basic factors are unchanged by the characters' actions. How the Supernaturals in *Last Ditch* came to be thus, what if anything it might mean to be created as such and whether or not they might be bound to continue in their current state, we, and they, are not to know. Their condition is given, and remains unaffected at the end of the play, leaving the world in a not-uncharacteristically unstable position. In addition, the very excess of the claims made for the intervention of the Supernaturals_in the lives of the Mayflies, plus the ascription of the ultimate power to transform the world to The Lynx of Meri Wells, tends to obscure that which *has* been transformed by the play. Even as Tanwen departs to fulfil her renewed sense of mission as an activist, we are left with a sense that Supernatural normalcy will be restored, and will outlast even the most determined Mayfly's flight. Similarly, despite their merciless James Bond-like fighting energy, the figures in *Land of My Fathers* do not effect change in their wider circumstances: their odyssey, including Iestyn's death, leaves no mark on the industrial system which allowed them to pursue it; and we are not a party to any effect which their disappearance might have on the state espionage agency. Though the action of both plays has some profound consequences for some of the (human) individuals involved, then, it is almost as if the premise of either play could be revisited, again and again, without disruption.

Another crucial part of sitcom's formal structure as drama is its industrial context, and to read these plays – particularly *Land of My Fathers* – as sitcoms is to allow for the incursion of industrial systemisation into the works and their vision. Historically speaking, the features of sitcom were established, and have been constantly adjusted throughout time, by the interests and capacities of the television industry, the systems of production and the reception of the product by the audience. Whatever the content of any individual story, it will be partly a reflection of imperatives beyond the reach of its immediate narrative and dramatic proposition. Moreover, this is known and acknowledged by the audience themselves, given that, as Mills (2005) notes, sitcoms 'contain material which can be read as conforming to generic structures; and audiences make sense of texts by comparison to genre expectations' (26). In that sense it is not dissimilar to the condition of the characters in *Land of My Fathers*: although actually MI6 agents, they present themselves as private security personnel, outsourced commercial staff working beyond the remit of government or military regulations. As Rabey himself notes in the Foreword to this publication, outsourcing forces 'a distance in time and space between action and consequences', normalizing and concealing long-term catastrophic human disposability, in order to establish and maintain a systematic short-term profitability' (Rabey, this volume: 144). For the great majority of the play, we experience the characters as being functionally indistinguishable from the bodies which assign them their mission, a fact which is enforced from the very beginning by the homage to James Bond in terms of the scenography of the original production.

Finally, sitcom traditionally operates in a domestic context, as Jones (1992) emphasises when programmatically defining the basic action of the genre as 'domestic harmony… threatened when a character develops a desire that runs counter to the group's welfare' (3). Thus, and with the proviso that we may define the realm of *Last Ditch*'s Supernaturals as a kind of *domus*, Annie's quest to stop M's malign practice of disconnection works not only as a plotline but also as a comic take on the clash of Apollonian and Dionysian forces which Nietzsche identifies as the source of tragic drama. What emphasises the domestic in terms of drama even more than this, however, is the formulaic use of language in the early Nigredo scenes of *Last Ditch* (Rabey, this volume: 23-46), where the same basic utterances find different resonances and contexts in different mouths from scene to scene: 'This is the beginning of the end' / 'Can we do this?' / 'We can't not.' / 'You're making me do this' / 'I shall let them down' . This repetition in the Mayflies' words suggests an absurdist dimension to the action until the transcendent world of the Supernaturals is suddenly introduced, first by Boneblack and then by the opening scene of the Albedo section with its comically – and poetically very different – set of conflicts between fixed characters.

In Nietzsche, humanity is broadly to be understood as bridging different states traditionally seen as contradictory, particularly good and evil. And so, however the plays formulate and formalise the division between the superterranean and subterranean worlds of outsourced contracting and hellscape gallery, or the ‘upstairs’ and ‘downstairs’ worlds of Supernaturals and Mayflies, the human is framed as a journey through and between both realms. In Rabey’s previous plays, that journey between was injected with the power and danger of sexual desire as a narcotic agent; but here – and especially in *Last Ditch* – the prevailing mood and agency of change is set by the pervasive *agreeability* of Annie and the cartoon-like mischief of The Lynx. Motivated though she may be to bring the Mayflies to a greater sense of occupying their own lives, such is the flightiness of her self-expression that she appears not to be entirely serious, or at the very least happily uncalculating in her action; finding her mission, as she puts it, ‘BOSTIN’ brilliant’ (Rabey, this volume: 100). As for The Lynx (like Zarathustra), he may claim that his great transformation can happen only once, the little scamp. But that’s what everybody says in sitcom…

Roger Owen as Dyfrig in *Last Ditch*. Photo: Hubert Sikorski.

REFERENCES:

Artaud, Antonin (1993) *The Theatre and its Double*. London: Calder Publications.

Barker, Howard (1993) *Arguments for a Theatre*. Manchester: Manchester University Press.

Baudrillard, Jean (2002) *The Spirit of Terrorism*. London: Verso.

Beckett, Samuel (2009) *Endgame*. London: Faber.

Jones, Gerard (1992) *Honey, I'm Home! Selling the American Dream*. New York: St Martin's Press.

Mills, Brett (2005) *Television Sitcom*. London: BFI.

Mintz, Larry (1985) '*Situation Comedy*' in B. G. Rose (ed.) TV Genres: A Handbook and Reference Guide. Westport, CT: Greenwood Press.

Nietzsche, Friedrich Wilhelm (2001) *Thus Spake Zarathustra*. Blacksburg, VA: Virginia Tech.

Rabey, David Ian (2004) *The Wye Plays*. Bristol: Intellect.

(2008) *Lovefuries*. Bristol: Intellect Books.

Shakespeare, William (1994) *King Lear*. London: Routledge (Arden Shakespeare).

Summer 2020: Annie crosses over into Downstairs. She's been talking to Iona Greenslade..(Photo by Ella Doheny)

Notes on Contributors

DAVID IAN RABEY was born in the Black Country of England, has lived in California and Dublin, and now lives in Machynlleth in Cymru/Wales, where he has resided since 1985 (and now identifies as Cymraeg/Welsh). He is a graduate of the Universities of Birmingham and California, Berkeley, and is Emeritus Professor of Drama and Theatre Practice at Aberystwyth University, where he taught from 1985 to 2020. He is Artistic Director of Lurking Truth/Gwir sy'n Llechu Theatre Company, which he co-founded in 1986, and for which he has written and/or directed the plays *The Back of Beyond* (staged twice 1996) and *The Battle of The Crows* (staged 1998), which are published together as *The Wye Plays* (2004); and *Bite or Suck* (staged 1997) and the double bill *Lovefuries* (*The Contracting Sea* and *The Hanging Judge*)(staged 2004 and 2005), published together as *Lovefuries* (2008). His critical writings include *Alistair McDowall's* Pomona (2018), *Theatre, Time and Temporality* (2016), *The Theatre and Films of Jez Butterworth* (2015), *Howard Barker: Ecstasy and Death* (2009), *English Drama Since 1940* (2003), *David Rudkin: Sacred Disobedience* (1997) and *Howard Barker: Politics and Desire* (1989). His work as a cinematographer includes Charmian Savill's short film *Spinfoam* (2024: Lurking Truth/Beady Films).

LARA MALEEN KIPP was born in Bavaria, Germany, and first moved to Wales for a Joint Honours BA in Scenography & Theatre Design and Drama & Theatre Studies at Aberystwyth University. Succumbing to the particular pull of said town, she subsequently pursued an MA in Practising Theatre & Performance, and then a PhD, engaging in an aesthetic analysis of Howard Barker's scenography, published as a monograph with Routledge in 2020. After a short stint in the Midlands as lecturer in Performing Arts (Drama) at the University of Derby, she returned to Aberystwyth where she now lectures at the university across drama and theatre, theatre design, and production design. She has published academic work with Intellect, Taylor & Francis, De Gruyter, and Palgrave Macmillan, among others. Her research interests range from scenography (costume in particular) and vocal performance to contemporary European and feminist theatres. Alongside academic endeavours, she engages in freelance scenographic work, including collaborative creative research with Eira Dance Theatre (formerly The Motion Pack).

PIOTR WOYCICKI is a Lecturer in Theatre and New Media at Aberystwyth University. His research interests concern the intersections between political and aesthetic theory and contemporary intermedial performance practice. He is the author of *Post-cinematic Theatre and Performance* (2014) and has published in various academic journals. His practice-as-research encompasses music composition and digital scenography design.

ROGER OWEN was born in Cardigan, Ceredigion, and is a Lecturer in Theatre and Theatre Production at Aberystwyth University, Wales UK. His teaching centres on acting, directing and theatre production, along with Welsh-medium theatre and drama and Performance Studies. His published research work includes *Writers of Wales: Gwenlyn Parry* (2013) and *Ar Wasgar* [Dispersed'], a historical study of Welsh language theatre and identity between 1979-97. He has worked as a performer with Brith Gof, Eddie Ladd and Lurking Truth/ Gwir sy'n Llechu: including the roles of Edgar in *The Back of Beyond*, Fury in *Lovefuries: The Hanging Judge* and Dyfrig in *Last Ditch (Anhrefn yng Nghymru*). He was dramaturg for Theatr Genedlaethol Cymru's production *Dawns Ysbrydion* (2015), and he is a regular theatre reviewer for the Welsh language magazine *Barn*.

LURKING TRUTH/GWIR SY'N LLECHU THEATRE COMPANY

Besides the plays in this volume, Lurking Truth has staged David Ian Rabey's *The Back of Beyond* (1996), *The Battle of The Crows* (1998), *Bite or Suck* (1997) and *Lovefuries* (2004, 2005); the world premiere of Arnold Wesker's *Letter to Myself* (2004); Howard Barker's plays *Victory* (1986), *Don't Exaggerate* and *The Castle* (1986), and English-language premieres of *The Twelfth Battle of Isonzo* (directed by the dramatist, Ireland and Wales, 2001-2), *A Wounded Knife* (2009) and *The Forty (Few Words)* (2011, 2014); Peter Barnes's *The Bewitched* (1987); Heathcote Williams's *AC/DC* (1997). The company's first film is *Spinfoam* by Charmian Savill (co-production with Beady Films, 2024).

Management board: Martin Culliford (Chair), Alison Coleman, David Ian Rabey (Secretary and Artistic Director); Company Direction Nucleus: Maisie Baynham, Lara Maleen Kipp, Roger Owen, Charmian Savill. Associate Artists: Paula Gardiner, Richard Lynch, Eric Schneider.

www.ingramcontent.com/pod-product-compliance
Lightning Source LLC
Chambersburg PA
CBHW081216170426
43198CB00017B/2632